# PURSUE

# *ME*

## UNTIL YOU SEE

# *HER*

## Stacci B. McElveen

# DEDICATION

This book is dedicated to all women who have gone through abuse and rejection and suffer in silence. This abuse is often caused by their love ones. Know that life does bounce back after hurt, the pain of rejection, rape, and mistrust.

# DEDICATION

This book is dedicated to all women who have gone through abuse and rejection and suffer in silence. This abuse is often caused by their love ones. Know that life does bounce back after hurt, the pain of rejection, rape, and mistrust.

# ACKNOWLEDGEMENT

First, I acknowledge and give honor to my Lord and Savior, Jesus Christ, who is first in my life. Without God, I would be nothing.

I thank my friend, Latysha Coleman, who heard my dream and desires and felt it necessary to introduce me to Mrs. Joan T Randall.

Thanks to Mrs. Joan T Randall who pushed me to start and finish this book the very first time I met her. I appreciated her inspirational messages, which encouraged me to get through the process of writing my story and for the worship sessions during the writing challenge. She always reminded me that, "You own your own story, and no one can take that away from you." You are simply amazing!

Thank you to Leslie Cottrell Simonds for her words of inspiration, "Don't shut down your voice. Your ego can keep you from serving God's will. Don't belittle yourself. If you do, then you are belittling God."

To my Editor, Lynn Braxton, thank you for your expertise in the writing process and for not holding back on us. She gave us her heart for editing.

To the Sun group, Latysha Coleman, K.T. Hender, Janet L. Jacobs, Tamra T. Bush, and Deleisha Webb, for all of your help and encouragement.

Thank you to my backbone, my rock, my mom, Evangelist Flossie Brown, who shows me every day how strong she is and sets an example that with God, all things are possible.

Thank you to all of my siblings, other family members, and friends for your love and patience.

Thanks to my pastor and other influential men and women of God for words of encouragement.

To my children, Victor Scott Jr, Joshua Scott, Leroy McElveen 3rd, and Nyqwesha McElveen, and my god-children, Yatta Gayflor, Naomi Swinton, Allison Young, and Kelly Nesmith, I love you all.

Last but not least, thank you to my husband, Mr. Leroy McElveen Jr. You are my hero.

# CONTENTS

# INTRODUCTION

Feelings of being unloved, unwanted, and neglected can cause a person to seek attention in all the wrong places and cause them to end up being abused by people they love. Abuse will cause a person to isolate themselves into a corner, needing help, but sometimes too ashamed or embarrassed to ask. They do not want anyone to know they were beaten and are vulnerable. There comes a time in your life when you have to stand up and live. Once you have had enough of being abused and defeated, enough of walking around unhappy, enough of spilling anger onto your family, enough of being alone, enough of being bitter, and wanting to live victorious, wanting love in your life, wanting to be free of being ME, and wanting to be HER, but it seems so hard, and you're unsure of what to do to get to that stage. You're crying because you can see HER, taste HER, dream about HER, but don't know how to get to HER. The "HER" who has moved on and is healed, eventually comes to the realization that the only person that can stop you from being the blessed you that you were destined to become, is you.

# SECTION I

# M E

# NEVER WILL BE THE SAME

When I entered the house, I sat on the couch. I heard footsteps coming down the steps, which was normal, but this time it was different. It was an uncomfortable feeling that made my stomach turn upside down. The thought of something unexplainable happening never crossed my mind. This action definitely caught me off guard. My heart was racing, but I didn't know why. Suddenly, Spencer entered the room. He had a different look on his face. I asked him, "Are you ok? You look strange?"

Spencer said in a crazy voice, "I'm going to bust your cherry."

His appearance caught my eyes as my left eyebrow went up. I noticed that he had changed clothes. He had on grey jogging pants that hugged him in the front. The imprint of his penis was showing. I wondered why he was bulging like that since we were just friends. It didn't register in my brain the unthinkable was getting ready to happen. I was so oblivious.

Of course, I laughed because I was not a virgin, but I had vowed I would not have sex with anyone except my future husband, my king. My focus is on serving God, because that's more important than fulfilling temporary desires. I, also, wanted to concentrate on my college classes. So, I didn't want any distractions that relationships can bring.

As Spencer came closer to me, I began to get nervous and confused. I jumped to my feet and quickly headed towards the door and said firmly, "Let's go!" He suddenly grabbed my arm and threw me on the floor. I hit my head hard, but not hard enough to where I could not fight. "What are you doing?" I said, as I bit his chest so hard that I knew he was going to bleed, but that didn't seem to bother him.

Spencer slapped me hard and started yelling at me, "Stop moving! Stop moving!" I continued to move side to side, struggling to get loose. He grabbed my arms and pinned them to the floor. I tried to get him off of me, but he was too heavy. I could barely move. He glared at me and said, "If you move again, I am going to choke you to death."

Tears trickled down my face as I glared back at him, afraid to say another word. The thought of what was happening to me, had me in a state of shock and disbelief. He was my best friend, someone I called brother, someone who protected me, someone who had a girlfriend. Spencer was the only person I talked to about the pain I had gone through in high school with Marlin. In desperation, I pleaded with him to stop, but he didn't.

Uncontrollable tears poured down my face as he began to Rape me.

# THE ENCOUNTER

Two years later, I was sitting in my office. I glanced at my watch and realized it was getting late. It was time for me to meet my good friend, Shirlene, at the coffee shop to go over a business plan that needed some signatures before approval. Shirlene and I became good friends a long time ago after a counseling session I had with our mutual friend, Dr. Wright, who is a clinical psychologist. I ordered my favorite latte and Shirlene ordered regular coffee with six Splenda and six creams. Shirlene was a financial counselor that had written a grant for my new business venture.

As we walked to a table, we were laughing at me because I almost tripped with a hot latte in one hand and had my phone in the other. When we sat down, I spotted a young girl sitting in the corner crying her eyes out with a look of despair. We tried to ignore her because we were on a time schedule; but we could not help but to intervene, because I recognized that look of despair. I felt something pulling me toward this young lady, So I decided to go and try to comfort her. We went over to the lady and introduced ourselves. "Hello! My name is Madelene, and this is my friend, Shirlene," I said. "Are you okay? Can we help you?"

At first, the lady turned her head away from us, as if we were disturbing her. Her eyes were wide open, full of fear, with tears coming down her face. She appeared nervous. She kept looking over her shoulder. She seemed to be scared, as if she was hiding from someone.

"Ma'am, can I help you with anything? I spoke. Can I make a phone call for you? I know you don't know me, but I am concerned about you. Are you running from someone?

Without saying a word, the woman looked at me and rolled her eyes.

"Let's leave her alone," Shirlene said. So, we turned to walk back to our table.

"Wait! Wait! My name is Santos," the lady said. "I'm running away from my husband! For eight years, he physically and mentally abused me. I'm tired of getting beat, lied to, cheated on, and raped," she said, sounding exasperated, as tears trickled down her cheeks.

"I'm sorry for what you have been through," I said softly. "There comes a time in your life when you have just had enough of being abused and you're ready to live in peace. You have to ask yourself, 'Am I tired of everyday drama? Do I want to be happy?'"

Shirlene being a little feisty said, "Excuse me, ma'am, but is your husband dead somewhere? I would not let a man put his hands on me," she said, putting her hands on her hips. "Why are

8

you here crying? You should be home figuring out a way to get back at him."-Shirlene kept rambling on and on and on.

I interrupted her in a loud, frustrated voice, "Shirlene, everyone is not like you. Have some compassion."

Santos said, "I am so tired." She looked down at her hands. They were shaking. She began to cry hysterically.

I walked closer to her, took her hands in mine, and said, "If you are ready to fight for your life, I can help you. Do you think he is coming here?"

In a weak, raspy voice, Santos said, "No, he went to work. As soon as he left our house, I knew I had to leave. So, I just kept running for miles and didn't stop to rest until I saw this coffee shop."

I could see that her husband had her so jumpy that she constantly looked over her shoulder. "Can we sit and talk for a minute?" I asked.

"Yes," she said.

Santos began to explain that she had been trying to get away from her husband for about a year. She believed he sensed that she would try to leave him, because when he would go to work or leave the house, he would always take the car keys for both cars, the house keys, and her pocketbook, which had all of her money. She felt trapped, with no one to turn to. Santos said they lived in a brownstone house in the Brownsville, Brooklyn area, which was about five miles from the coffee shop in downtown Brooklyn.

I asked her, "Where are you going?"

With her head down, Santos replied sadly, "I don't have a clue. I was just going to run or walk until I could figure out something."

Santos began to tell us about her life. "My husband was not always abusive. Michael is his name. He's a bank teller at the Chemical Bank on the west side of Manhattan, which is where we met. I was a senior at the Fashion Institute of Technology college studying fashion merchandising when I first met him. I had dreamed of studying fashion trends and fashion products for retail stores."

"That's a great school," I said while I looked over at Shirlene rolling her eyes and hitting her watch because it was getting late.

Santos continued, "I was an intern at a local fashion merchant shop. They trusted me to make bank deposits and withdrawals. I felt really important. Michael would always make sure I came to his window. He would always flirt with me. I thought he was the most handsome man I had ever laid my eyes on."

Shirlene said, "Those good-looking men can fool you sometimes."

I hit her under the table and said, "Will you stop?"

Santos looked annoyed, "Listen, I know you are busy. So, don't worry about me. I can take care of myself. Thank you for your concern! You really made me feel better," she said as she got up from the table.

"No, you don't have to leave. I do have time for you. Don't worry about Shirlene. She can be rude sometimes. Go ahead, continue," I said as I gave Shirlene an evil eye.

"One Friday, he asked me on a date and that was history," Santos smiled. We dated for two years. I watched him move up in the banking industry as I was getting known in the fashion world. My intern job became a permanent job. That Thanksgiving we went to my parents' house in South Carolina. My mother and Michael arranged to have my whole family there. After dinner, he asked me if he could have a piece of cake. I said sure, let's go in the kitchen. My little brother was standing there with a card in his hand. He passed it to me. I read it. It said, 'Will you marry me?' I looked at Michael and he was holding a ring. I couldn't believe it! Of course, I said yes, because I really loved him."

"That was sweet," I said. Shirlene stepped on my foot under the table.

"After we were married for three years, I got pregnant. We were the happiest married couple that ever walked this earth, until I had a miscarriage. He asked me to stop working so he could take care of me. He told me that whenever I got pregnant again, he didn't want me stressed out, so I would be able to carry the next baby full-term. He thought the stress from the fashion job was the cause of the miscarriage."

Santos grabbed a tissue to wipe her eyes. Her voice sounded weak and low as she said, "The abuse started after we were having a hard time getting pregnant the second time. He told me that I was not worth anything, I was not a real woman."

As Santos continued to tell us what she had been experiencing in her life, the more I felt like I knew her and wanted to help her. My heart began to feel the hurt and pain she was feeling as I stared in her eyes and said, "You are beautiful! You are worthy, and you are a real woman."

"Santos, can I tell you my story? I said.

"Yes," she sobbed.

"Since I was not always happy with myself, I began seeking the wrong kind of attention. This led me into the arms of abusive men, including my ex-husband." Although Shirlene and I were good friends, I had never told her about my past.

# THE BEGINNING

It all started when I was a little girl who had to fight in order to be accepted by others. I come from a family of fifteen people, ten girls, three boys, plus my mom and dad. I was the eighth child. Being the middle child, I wasn't sure if I was supposed to act like the older children or the younger. My older brothers and sisters were bold. They would break curfew, knowing that breaking the house rules came with consequences. They felt like their crime (breaking curfew), was worth the time they had to spend on punishment. I wanted to be like my older brothers and sisters. However, at the same time, I wanted to be babied like the younger ones, because they always got away with everything.

We grew up in a four-bedroom apartment in the housing authority. Our bedrooms looked like an orphanage because of the bunk beds that lined the walls. We were poor because my father was the only one working.

"An Orphanage!" Shirlene and Santos said at the same time.

Yes, but it was not uncomfortable. We still had our own little space. Besides, we were young, and that was all we knew. My parents had such a strong relationship that if anything was wrong or if they didn't have money for bills, they still managed to seem happy. Their love seemed to carry them through any hardship. Growing up with no money didn't seem to be important, because love for family is what kept us together and made us strong.

When I was with my friends, I began to notice that adults would praise my peers and act so concerned about their day or their future, but would never ask me anything. Sometimes, they patted me on the head like a puppy without really looking at me or talking to me. They made me feel invisible. I would speak up and say, "Hello!" just to let them know I was there, only to continue to be ignored. Perhaps, it was because I didn't have on the latest clothes, or didn't have the longest hair, or because I didn't have parents with money in the bank. Regardless of the reason, they made me feel unwanted, unloved, and unliked.

When I went home and looked at myself in the mirror, I asked, "What is wrong with me? Why do people treat me the way they do?" Perhaps, it was because of my dark-brown skin and skinny body. Society would publicize light-skinned people as beautiful, while dark- or browned-skinned people were portrayed as undesirable, to the point where some dark or browned skinned people would bleach their skin to make themselves lighter. Often times, I wished I had the money to do the same, just so I could finally get attention.

Each time I was rejected by adults, my eyes would tear up and my heart would start pounding like it was going to burst out of my chest. This caused me to be jealous of my peers, almost to the point of losing my own identity and wanting to become other people. I would sometimes steal my sister's clothes or borrow clothing from my peers, just to pretend to be them and not myself.

To counter the feelings of being rejected, I became very competitive. I joined different organizations, such as the track club. My track coach saw my potential and said I could be in future Olympic games. So, he pushed me to the limit, always challenging me to compete with older, faster girls as a way of training me to be better and stronger. I, also, joined the debate teams which gave me a chance to demonstrate that being pushed around was not in my character. When it was time to rebut my opponent's argument, I was always ready with a response to defend my point of view. Being selected for cheerleading captain was one thing I had to fight for, because I was told I was not pretty enough. Yet, my team voted for me. Every organization I joined; I was very good at it. It felt great to hear the words, "You did good! or "Wow! You are awesome!" I felt in charge, empowered, and in control.

Over a period of time, I started feeling empty again, yearning for the feeling of acceptance and love from others. Joining different groups no longer satisfied me. That high was gone! It was as if I was on a drug and needed–something else stronger, needed another hit. I turned my focus to see how I could get boys to look my way. I began to flirt with every boy that said hello. I would even have sex with a few, only to feel empty afterwards. I really thought I found my new high. Boys began to tell me, "I love you." Those sweet lies rolling from their tongues into my inner ear was all I needed, at least that's what I thought. The words, "I love you," or "Girl, you are all of that," gave me a sense of comfort and protection thinking this person really meant every word, only to discover the word, love, was used to just to gain my trust and get in my panties. After they got what they wanted, I was no longer needed.

When I returned home after being with these boys, and figured out they didn't care about me, I felt ashamed and tears filled my eyes. Whenever I felt bad, I would go straight to my mirror to talk to Jesus, because that always seemed to comfort me. I asked the Lord, "Why do I keep falling into the same relationships that leave me broken and insecure?" With no responses from Jesus, I just stared in the mirror as thoughts ran through my mind that I had given those boys all my love and body thinking that was the way to show love, while expecting to receive love in return. I didn't realize that I was going to be disappointed once again because I was out of order according to the bible.

Each time my heart was broken by a relationship, it added more weight on my shoulders. At times, it felt like I was carrying a heavy load of bricks on my back with no relief. I found myself taking my frustration out on my siblings. I would yell or belittle them for no reason; often camouflaging what was really going on inside of me. I knew their love would always be there, no matter what, because they had unconditional love for me.

# MY FIRST LOVE

In high school, I dated a young man named Marlin who was a short, light-skinned, yummy looking guy with muscles all over his body. I saw him at a house party but pretended not to pay him any attention. All the girls were throwing themselves at him because he was a show stopper with his looks and his dancing. The D.J. played one of my favorite songs called, "It Takes Two," by Rob Base & DJ EZ Rock. I wanted to chill for the night, but my friends knew I was an amazing dancer. They loved to see me show out. So, I got on the dance floor and did my thing. The crowd began screaming my nickname, "GO MAD! GO MAD!" until it caught Marlin's attention. He suddenly jumped behind me and tried to outshine me, but I showed him that I was not a two-step dancer. To his amazement, I was so good that I put him to shame in front of his friends.

After the dance battles, the crowd calmed down when the D.J. began to play a Jamaican song called, "Everyone Hustle," by Josey Wales. As everyone coupled-up to dance, girls were coming to him to dance because he was known to give girls organisms while dancing Jamaican style. To my surprise, he turned everyone down and grabbed my arm and asked me to dance with him. I smiled and nodded. He pulled me close to him as he was grinding, and his hands were all over my body. It was very stimulating.

He whispered in my ear, "What's your name?"

"Madelene," I said in my sexiest voice.

"There is something different about you."

"What do you mean?"

"You are not like these other gold-digging girls. You seem to have this purity about you. I want to get to know you better," Marlin whispered.

First of all, I could not believe someone that looked as good as him wanted someone that looked like me. The attention he gave me was exceptional, incredible, and hallucinatory, because things like this just didn't happen to me. To get the attention of the most popular guy made me feel special, important, and finally visible.

Two weeks later we had our first official date at an amusement park called Great Adventures. We had a lot of fun. Marlin kept telling me that he finally found his match and he was never going to let me go. Our connection was electric because we had a lot in common. He loved to dance, and I loved to dance. He was funny and I was funny. He loved bowling and I loved bowling. We became so close that our nickname was M & M. My friends envied our relationship. He would leave his school every day and drive across town to pick me up from my school. He would give me money to buy what I wanted. My peers would tell me that I was the luckiest girl in the world, guys like him do not come around often. Being with him, changed me, he made me feel confident and special. I loved the attention he gave me.

Shirlene interrupted and said, "You still like attention." Which made Santos smile a little.

I turned my head and said, "Really, can I finish?"

"You may, but remember we are on a schedule," Shirlene said sarcastically.

"How can I forget with you tapping your watch every few minutes?" I said, as we all laughed.

Anyway, Marlin would always have at least a thousand dollars on him each week. I knew because being curious, I would look in his wallet to see how much money he had. Every time he gave me money, it was at least three hundred dollars. He didn't have a job, but I never questioned where he got the money from. I just knew that I could finally buy designer clothes. Now, I would be accepted by my peers. I would later find out that the money and the attention I received came with a price.

After dating Marlin for about six months, we became intimate. With all those dance moves, my curiosity was right, he knew how to satisfy. Our first time was very special and not planned. We were at his house in his room, like we always were, just playing Uno, laughing, and having a great time. Then, the radio played, "You are my Lady," by Freddie Jackson. Marlin looked at me with tears in his eye and said, "Madelene, I never thought I could love someone as much as I love you." At that moment, my heart was filled with joy because someone finally understood what I wanted. He began to kiss me, and the rest of the evening was magical.

It was not long after that when he became possessive, controlling and abusive. At our age, we should have friends of both genders, but if I was caught holding a conversation with a guy, Marlin would flip out. Guys were scared to speak to me, because he had people looking out for him at my school.

On one occasion our political science teacher split the class up in groups to do a group project on the different political parties and my group consisted of two boys and two girls, and I explained to Marlin that my group had boys and we had to work together to get a good grade. Marlin acted as if he understood what I had to do, and I could be trusted. Right after school, my group met at the library to discuss our strategy. Shortly into our planning session, I was surprised to see Marlin had showed up and began to make a scene. He put his arms around my neck and looked at my classmates with an evil eye and said, "Stay away from my girl." He had a reputation of being a bad boy or thug, and people stayed out of his way. Both guys and girl in my group got up and walked away and went to the adjacent table. They continued meeting daily on the project without me, but included me in the verbal presentation, even though all I had to do was read what was written on the poster board.

When we planned on meeting somewhere to eat, or if Marlin told me to come to his house, he gave me a time he thought I should be there. If I arrived later than he expected, he would jump in my face and yell, "What took you so long?" He treated me as if I was a child. If I talked back to him, he would intimidate me by clinching his jaws tight while staring at me for a long time without blinking his eyes. Soon, physical abuse became very common. He slapped me each time we went out for reasons such as asking if he would turn the music down. If I didn't feel like having sex with him whenever he was ready, he would get very upset and accuse me of sleeping with other men while yelling and calling me a slut or whore. It was not easy being in a relationship with him. I was far from happy.

As time went by, I wanted to get out of this relationship, because I was tired of his abuse. It was hard getting away from Marlin because he became a stalker. Everywhere I went with my family or friends, he would suddenly show up unannounced. He would give excuses, such as he just wanted to make sure I got home safe or just wanted to see who I was talking to. I never understood how he knew where I was all the time, unless he had me followed. He sometimes popped up at my house. I would act as if I knew he was coming, but had forgotten to tell my parents, because they did not like surprise guests. Marlin would leave his high school early just to come to my school and watch me. I didn't find out until later that he was watching my every move and checking to see what I was wearing. Although I was scared of him, I was even more afraid to tell anyone, because I knew somebody might get killed because of me; I didn't want that on my conscience. I was stuck in a bad situation and needed a way out. I was too young to go through this. Was the attention-seeking worth this nightmare?

"What grade were you in when this was going on?" Santos inquired.

"A junior in high school," I responded.

Continuing with my story, I told Shirlene and Santos that I had a mother that made us pray with her every Sunday morning before church service. While she was praying, I thought to myself, "God, if you can hear me, please help me." As we prayed and prayed, the vision of me being free from Marlin appeared in my mind.

When I was by myself, I cried my eyes out in fear of him because it was not easy getting away from him. He came from a thuggish, gang banging family that was about the life of kill or be killed. I had some family members that was about that life as well, so I remained silent.

A week later, unknowingly my prayers were answered.

While we were outside waiting for cheerleading practice to start, a strange young man walked toward me and my friends. He called me by my name and asked to speak to me in private. He beckoned for me to come to where he was standing, making sure to distance himself from my friends. I looked at him as if he was crazy, because first of all I didn't know him and second,

22

I had no clue if Marlin was watching me, so I ignored him. This stranger walked closer towards me and spoke in a soft deep voice, "It's about your boyfriend, Marlin." Now, he had my attention. Once he mentioned Marlin's name, it felt like everything around me stopped. I noticed that he was a short light-skinned guy that had on dark blue jeans, a black hoody, white Air-max Nike sneakers, with gold teeth.

"Who is that? Hook a sister up?" Sylvia, my co-captain for cheer, said jokingly.

I looked at her and said, "I have no clue who he is, but I will try."

I was afraid to walk toward him, my legs were trembling, and my heart was beating fast. I wasn't sure what he wanted. What if my boyfriend Marlin was watching from a distance? Nonetheless, I decided to hear what he had to say. In a bold voice I said, "Who are you and how do you know me?"

"You don't have to worry about who I am. Just know that I know who you are, and you never have to worry about your boyfriend again," retorted the stranger.

"What do you mean?" I inquired.

"His family had to suddenly leave town. We saw how he was treating you and thought you should know."

I took a step back and repeated, "What do you mean?" "Where is he?" "What happened?

The unnamed guy walked towards me, put his hand on my shoulder, looked me in the eyes, and said, "Like I said, you don't have to worry about him anymore."

Once he removed his hands from my shoulder, a weight seemed to lift off me. Yet, I was confused about where he had come from and how long he had been watching me and Marlin. My mind started to flutter with all kinds of thoughts. "Who is this guy?" "Where is Marlin?" "Why did he suddenly leave without contacting me? Nevertheless, the feeling of freedom overwhelmed me as I began to shed tears. I wanted to ask one more question, but the strange man was gone.

My friends came over to hug me and began asking questions. "Who was that guy? Why are you crying? If he knew who your boyfriend was, he would not have made you cry."

Wiping the tears from my eyes, I answered, "It's nothing." I thought to myself again, *How did this man know who I was? Who was he and how did he know what school I attended?* Either way I was happy and free. No more of the physical and mental abuse, it was time to heal those scars. I didn't even try to verify the information, I just believed it was true. When I got home from school, there was a news clip of a shooting near where Marlin lived, and the shooter was still at large. I assumed it must have involved his family.

I decided to leave relationships alone and focus on just having fun, friends, and earning some money. I got a job at the local department store and was just happy as a young girl could be.

I knew in my heart I had gone through a lot. It was time to heal and heal properly. So, one evening I went to bible study with my mom. The pastor was teaching on Proverbs 18:22 which says, "Who so ever findeth a wife findeth a good thing, and obtaineth favor of the Lord." I pulled out the mirror that was in my pocketbook, looked in the mirror and said, "*Yes, I am a good thing.*" I have been going about this the wrong way. Now I understand my value, my worth. So, when I meet my future husband, I pray he will value me as a "good thing" like the bible says.

At that point I dedicated my life to Jesus Christ, joined the church, sang in the choir, joined the usher board, and was one of the personal secretaries to the pastor. Staying busy in the church was my safe haven as well as my comfort zone.

During our annual church meetings, a lot of young people my age wanted to get to know each other. We were enjoying each other as young people and trying to figure out life. Being with someone was the last thing on my mind. Pursuing God and my dreams of becoming an inspirational speaker, mentor for women, and an accountant were my goals. I was happy.

# THE MIRROR LIED

Every morning when I looked in the mirror, I saw a round-face pecan image with big eyes that appeared to have all the confidence in the world, but in reality, there was a look of gloom and unhappiness in the reflection in front of me. The mirror told me that I was beautiful, but on the inside of my soul was a little girl crying, because what I saw in front of me didn't seem real. I battled with the pain of my past and the negative things that caused me to believe my life was nothing. It was like a cymbal with no sound. I felt like I was just here to take up space until the Lord comes to get me. In the mirror, I saw the woman I wanted to be, but I knew the fight and the process was going to be so hard to get to that image, that I became comfortable in "just living."

Looking in the mirror and drowning in my thoughts and imagination, I thought I heard the mirror say, "*Go into the world and conquer it since you are dressed for the part.*" I didn't feel strong enough to conquer anything. I was tired from constantly having to battle with my surroundings and feelings of being left out and taken advantage of. All I ever wanted was to be loved and appreciated.

In front of the mirror was where I felt I could be myself. I would stand in front of it while reading the Holy Bible each day. It comforted me and gave me strength in the comfort of my home. The verse that gave me confidence that everything was going to work out is Romans 8:28 which says, "And we know that all things work together for the good to them that love God, to them who are the called according to his purpose." But outside of my home, fear and doubt crept into my mind and made me think that things would not work out for my good because of the things that had happened to me.

*"YOU ARE PRECIOUS AND GOD CHOSE YOU TO BE A LEADER. HE CHOSE YOU TO STAND OUT AND STAND UP,"* the mirror seemed to scream at me.

Frustrated, I said, "But how, when the past hurts so much?"

# A SAFE PLACE

Shirlene reminded me, again, that we were on a time schedule and we needed to get the papers signed so that she could deliver them to the federal government before five o'clock. So, we excused ourselves to sign the papers.

"Hey Santos! do you have a place to go? What are your plans?" I inquired.

"With no money and no family in the area," Santos chuckled, "I was going to find a shelter, because going back to my husband right now is not an option. I just need to get away for a while and don't want him to find me."

"Wait a minute! Let me and Shirlene handle this business and I will help you." Santos looked at me with gratitude and said, "Thank you," with a smile and relief on her face.

After signing the papers, I pulled out my phone and began to make phone calls to various women's shelters to see if they had room for Santos. Each shelter stated that they would not have a bed available until next week or next month.

After pondering in my mind what else to do. I remembered Dr. Crystal Brown, an old friend, owed me a favor. Dr. Brown was over a woman's shelter ministry about two hours away. Her program offered protected identity, security, counseling, job placement, and the love of a family. This facility was like a gated community that had ten different houses with eight women per house. Each room was a master bedroom, big enough for a couch, and had its own bathroom. All the women shared the kitchen, dining room, large laundry room with three washing machines and three dryers, and a living room.

The phone rang three times before Dr. Brown answered. When she realized it was me, she sounded surprised, but happy. "Hey, Madelene! Longtime since I heard from you. How are you? How are the husband and children? We have to go out to dinner to catch up on our lives."

"Everything is great. My family is well, no complaints, and yes, we have a lot to talk about, Dr. Brown."

Dr. Brown said, "Call me Crystal, you know you are not just my client; you are my friend."

I laughed, "Ok, Doc."

"Girl, you are still funny. Anyway, how can I help you?"

"I met this young lady in the neighborhood coffee shop. She doesn't have any money, no place to go, and was running from her abusive husband. I was wondering if you could help her. She is very terrified to go back home."

"Well, at this time, I don't have a space available, however, there will be some spaces in about two weeks. Can you get her somewhere safe until then?" Dr. Brown replied.

"No, I've called every shelter close by and they are all booked up."

"Madelene, do you think you can take her home with you while I try to work out something?" asked Dr. Brown.

Stepping away from Santos so she couldn't hear my conversation, I said, "My house!"

"Yes, Madelene, you have that guest house. It will only be for a short while. Remember, as a favor for you, I will be putting her ahead of my long list of women who need my services, too." Dr. Brown ended our conversation by saying, "We are our sisters' keeper."

I took a deep breath and said, "Indeed, you are right. I couldn't live with myself if something happens to her, and I didn't do my best to help."

Dr. Brown said, "Great! Once you get Santos safe, call me back because I want to start her paperwork."

Santos was now on the top of the list. Dr. Brown's ministry blessed abused women everywhere and helped them in their growth towards becoming self-sustaining by helping to build their confidence with all the tools needed to live a better life, such as teaching them how to create a budget, how to perform well during a job interview, and most importantly how-to live-in peace.

Once I got home, I introduced Santos to the family as a friend that was going to stay with us in the guest house for a couple of weeks. My husband, Johnny, looked at me strangely because he knew I didn't really know Santos. He often said I had a heart of gold and that I was always lending a helping hand to anyone who needed it. However, I had never brought a stranger to our home.

Johnny and I had been married ten years. He's my second husband. When we met, I was in a very good place mentally. He married a woman that knows who and what she is in life. I am his second wife. My husband politely asked to talk to me in private. When we got in the bedroom, Johnny looked at me with an inquisitive stare and said, "You just met this lady, didn't you? Tell me what's going on with her before I say yes to her staying here, in our home."

I explained, "She was running from her abusive husband and all the shelters were booked up. Our friend, Dr. Brown, suggested that she come home with me for a couple of weeks until she has space for her in her facility."

With concern in his eyes he said, "Okay, but her husband better not come to our house disturbing our peace. I'm going to support you this time, but in the future call me and we will arrange something else. You are such a great wife and person. This must be really serious."

"Yes, it is," I replied.

We walked back to the television room. My husband looked at Santos and said, "Welcome to our home. Are your bags in the car?"

I jumped in and said before she could answer, "No, she only has what you see. But since we're about the same size, I'm sure I have some clothes that can fit her."

After dinner, it was time to show Santos where she was going to be sleeping. Santos was in "awe" because the guest house was decorated so beautifully. It was like a one-bedroom apartment with all the appliances. I reassured her that she was going to be safe here.

The next morning, I called Dr. Brown so we could get Santos's paperwork started. Dr Brown was on speaker phone. I heard her ask Santos if she was ready for a change or did she just want a place to cool off for a while and then return to her abusive husband. Dr. Brown made it clear that she was not going to place anyone in her shelter who was just looking for a temporary change. Her residents had to want a permanent change, not just for a place to live, but a change in their mindset, and a willingness to rejuvenate their body, and soul. She explained that Santos may need to relocate or reconnect with family members who may be able to provide a safe place for her long term.

Santos said, "I am ready for a change." Santos handed me the phone and said Dr. Brown wanted to talk to me.

Dr. Brown told me that as she was talking to Santos, she was checking her criminal record, and she is clear. Dr. Brown said that it might be two days to two weeks before placing her at the site.

Both Santos and I were so excited for her new life to come.

As I turned to go back into my home, Santos suddenly said, "Wait! Tell me more about your story. How did you get to where you are now?"

I yawned and said, "Get some rest! You've had a trying day, and I'm tired, too. We'll talk more tomorrow. Good night!"

# THE BETRAYAL

The next morning was Saturday, and Shirlene came over as she always does for our weekly two-hour workout session. After our exercise session, we sat down, and Santos came to join us.

"Y'all look like that work out was painful," Santos laughed.

"It was," I said as I grabbed the towel and grunted in pain.

"You are showing your age Madelene," said Shirlene.

We burst out in laughter.

"Madelene, how did you get to this place of happiness? You look so peaceful," Santos said. "You are enjoying life. I want to experience what you have. Can you continue telling me your story and how you got to a place of being happy in your life?"

"You thought about that all night?"

"Yes, Madelene, because you look well put together."

"Sure, first let me make us some tea and finger sandwiches, because I'm hungry," I said.

While I was in the kitchen, the laughter from the ladies in the backyard was so uplifting. It felt good to see Santos smiling and laughing. Even though I had just met her yesterday, it seems as though she has gone through some traumatic experiences. I'm glad that she feels safe in our home and is able to relax and exhale without worrying about her husband beating her.

The ladies were still laughing when I returned with the food. I asked, "What's so funny?"

"I was telling Santos about an incident that happened in church," chuckled Shirlene.

"Which incident?" I replied, as they continued to laugh.

"Remember that Sunday we were in church and the music was playing, and you were going through some personal things. When the organist hit that certain note on the keyboard, you started jumping up and down doing the holy dance and forgot you had loosened your draw string ponytail. Since it wasn't secure, it came flying off. That was not the funny part though. The funny part was when your son took your ponytail, put it on his head, and started imitating you," Shirlene shrieked with laughter.

"Of all the stories you could have told about me, why did you choose that one?"

"Because it was funny! Remember your little alfalfa hair was sticking up. On top of that, the elder and the people in the church were so distracted, that they lost focus of the spirit flowing through the church once they saw your hair," said Shirlene laughing uncontrollably.

All of us began to laugh. As we settled down, Santos looked at me and said, "How did you get to this happy place?"

"I went through some things that gave me the strength to stand."

"Can you tell me more about your life, the process you had to go through to get here?" inquired Santos.

"Sure, I can."

During my college days, I had met a young man named Spencer. He was good looking, but he wasn't my type. We went to York University together. He was a good friend. Spencer treated me like a little sister. He would pick me up from my house, and we would go to school and other places together. We had an understanding that we were just friends. He talked to me about his relationships. I would just listen and offer advice, but I really didn't have an answer, because it was none of my concern. After he would finish talking about his issues, the only wise thing to say was, "If you are not happy, then do something to make yourself happy." We were so close.

Spencer was the only person that knew about the physical abuse I had gone through during my younger years. I had even met his girlfriend, Kinsley, and we became friends, too. His girl knew that Spencer and my friendship was no threat to her. In fact, when the three of us went out bowling, to church, or other places, they would invite some guy to try to set me up. But it never worked out. My trust level was gone, and I was trying to heal from prior abusive relationships.

Well one day, Spencer called to tell me he was on his way to pick me up to hang out. He drove a white Oldsmobile Cutlass, with leather seats. His car was always clean and smelled new. Waiting with anticipation, the excitement of hanging out with my friend was euphoric. I never gave up the chance to hang with him. Since we were just friends, coming to pick me up at my door was never a requirement. So, when he drove up to my building and blew the horn, I went running down the stairs, opened the car door, and greeted him with excitement as always.

"Why are you so happy and hyper all the time, he asked?"

"Because I am happy," I smiled.

As we were driving and laughing at Eddie Murphy's standup comedy, "RAW."

Spencer said, "I have to go by the house because I forgot my wallet."

"You are always leaving something, if your head was not attached to your body, then you would leave that too" I chuckled. I was fine with it because it was normal for him to detour to other places before we got to our destination.

Spencer said, "Come in because it may take a while because I have to use to bathroom."

"No, I'll wait here in the car; it shouldn't take you that long, right?" I asked.

"It's hot and I'm not going to leave my car running, wasting gas. Just come inside the house for a minute."

"Ok, ok, since you insist, I'll come in." Since this was nothing out of the ordinary, I felt comfortable waiting for him in his house. I sat on the couch while he went upstairs. After a few minutes, I heard footsteps coming down the steps. Although this was normal, something seemed different this time. I suddenly felt uneasy. My heart was racing, but I didn't know why. When he came down the stairs, Spencer had a strange look on his face. Sitting on the couch I looked up at him. He looked different, almost deranged. I didn't recognize this person that stood in front of me.

"Spencer, are you ok? You look strange?"

He stood there looking down at me and with a mean, demanding, scary voice snarled, "I'm fine, but I'm about to be better in a few minutes, because today I'm going to bust your cherry."

"Bust my cherry! What are you talking about? Stop playing around. Let's go!"

I noticed that he had changed clothes. He had on grey jogging pants that hugged him in the front. The imprint of his penis was showing. I was caught off-guard. I wondered why he was bulging like that since we were just friends. It didn't register in my brain the unthinkable was getting ready to happen. I was so oblivious.

I laughed and added, "Although I am not a virgin, you know that I'm not having sex with anyone because I vowed to wait for my future husband. Besides, serving God and getting to know myself has more benefits at this stage in my life while I wait to be found by my husband." He moved closer to me and I began to get nervous.

"I'm not playing with you. You're mine today," he said firmly.

I was confused. I jumped up and headed quickly towards the door and, said, "LET'S GO!" as loudly as I could.

Spencer grabbed my arm, and threw me down, banging my head hard on the floor, but not hard enough to knock me out where I couldn't still fight.

"What are you doing?" I screamed.

I bit his chest so hard that I knew he was going to bleed, but that didn't make him stop. He slapped me so hard that my lips began to jiggle up and down. He started yelling, "Stop moving, stop moving!" I was moving side to side with as much force as I could muster, trying to get him off of me. With all the strength that I had, I tried to use my legs and hips to push him off. I balled up my hands into a fist and began to pound on his back like a drum. I was in the fight of my life.

Spencer grabbed my arms and pinned them to the floor so I couldn't move my arms. and positioned his legs inside of my legs giving me less ability to move.

"If you move again, I am going to choke you to death," he said enraged.

I was in shock because I knew what was going to happen. I was in disbelief, because Spencer was my best friend. Someone I called brother. Someone who had always protected me. Someone who had a girlfriend. He was the only person that knew about the pain I had gone through in high school with Marlin. I began to cry uncontrollably, as I pleaded with him to stop.

He loosened the gripped off of my left arm to use his hand to pull down his sweatpants. I remembered seeing a knife on the table next to my head. I tried to get it, but he grabbed it and pressed it against my neck. He was outraged and said, "I will slice your neck if you don't stop moving." He put the knife down, but out of my reach.

"Why Spencer? I don't understand. I never acted like I wanted you in this way. You were supposed to protect me." I sobbed.

He said nothing.

With all of his weight pressed against me, Spencer tugged at my pants and pulled them down, revealing my brown thighs. He ripped my shirt as if he was the Incredible Hulk. He began sucking on my breast. He grabbed and gripped me tightly. Is he drunk? I thought. What was going on? Am I really getting raped by my best friend? He pulled down my panties, pulled down his grey jogging pants, and began to penetrate me. He started breathing heavily as he picked up the pace. The sweat of his brow dripped on my smooth pecan skin as tears steadily flowed from my eyes.

Spencer whispered "Do, you like it? "

"NO! NO! PLEASE STOP!" I cried out with anger.

"Shut up, you know you love this," he claimed.

I laid still with fear that he would hurt me, if I tried anything. The feeling of him moving in and out of me wasn't right! He was hurting me both physically and emotionally. As he began to speed up, I knew he was about to reach his climax. I was hoping he wouldn't ejaculate in me. As he was pounding against me, he began to kiss my face and bite my neck. I couldn't stop crying. I begged him to stop, but to no avail.

"Please, please stop. Take me home," I pleaded.

Spencer picked up the knife from the table and pointed it at me again and stated, "You better listen to me."

As I lay there afraid, I realized I could hear the sound of footsteps upstairs. I began to scream as loud as I could, hoping someone would come to my rescue!

"Shut up! No one is going to help you," he snarled. "I'll stab you if you don't be quiet."

He wasn't in the right frame of mind. What gave him the idea that I was that type of chick? The nerve of him hurting me like this. My heart was filled with pain and disappointment as tears continued to fall down my face.

As I looked up, I saw a mirror on the ceiling of his living room. All the feelings of being unwanted, unloved, emotions of distrust, rape, abuse came flooding over me. I kept looking in the mirror as he was doing his thing. I began talking to God, even though I was in distress. I cried out, "God! Help me, please!" I continued crying uncontrollably. In the stillness of my spirit, I heard a voice say, "*Vengeance is mine!*" I just lay there numb.

When he finished, not once, but twice, he said gruffly, "Go clean yourself up so I can take you home." He acted as if I was cheap or disgusting. I got up and grabbed my pants. He threw me a shirt that was on the chair since he had ripped my shirt. As I was putting on his shirt, I was and angry and frustrated, because even after all of what happened, I had to allow him to take me home because there was no public transportation nearby.

On the way home it was silent in the car, until Spencer said, "If you tell anyone what happened, I will deny it."

I could not speak or move, because I was still in a state of shock. When we got close to my house, I jumped out of the moving car and ran as fast as I could away from Spencer, that lying rapist, my enemy, my hero, who became my zero. I was so angry! He really hurt me, my pride, and took away the little trust I had in people. I felt like the body I was in was not mine.

Once in my house, the only thing on my mind was to run straight to the bathtub, rub all of his scent off of me, and try to forget what happened. I sat on the edge of the tub and turned the water on. The thought of what happened kept playing over and over again in my mind. I could still feel him on top of me. I was staring at the water as if in a trance, angry that this had happened to me. I had forgotten the water was still running until it started spilling over the tub, wetting my pants and the floor. I slowly pulled my pants off. The smell of him was so strong, that it made my stomach turn upside down. I threw my pants and his shirt in the trash. Then laid in the tub and cried and prayed, then cried and prayed some more.

Once I felt clean on the outside, ensuring the smell of him had been washed off, I dried myself off with a towel. I walked past the mirror and wept out of control. I felt so stupid, naïve, and confused. I asked the mirror, *"Why did Spencer forsake me? GOD, WHY DID YOU ALLOW MY FRIEND TO RAPE ME?"* There was no response. With unrestrained tears flowing down my face once again, I stared at the image in the mirror. It was a broken reflection of ME.

When I got home, I was glad no one was there, because I would have to answer a lot of questions such as, *"Why are you taking a bath in the middle of the day? Why are you crying? What happened to your shirt? You left with Spencer? Where is He?"*

For days I stayed in the house, because I couldn't face anyone after what happened to me. This was unusual for me, because I always enjoyed getting out of the house. Every day I walked past the mirror and glanced at my reflection. The mirror portrayed my outer beauty, but inside I was broken. I was destroyed and distraught. When anyone asked if everything was alright, I would smile and say, "Yes, I'm fine," which was the opposite of what I was really feeling.

I held in my anger around my family as best I could, but there were times I lashed out at my siblings for nothing. My brothers would say, "Oh, Lord, she has PMS again." When I was alone, left with my flesh and my thoughts of that event, rage played back in my mind. The thought of being raped, made me feel as if I had fire in my eyes. My skin felt like it was boiling hot, and if I touched it, I imagined my fingers would burn. I had a strong desire to get revenge. In the ghetto, you would first get even, then call the cops. I walked back and forth, crying and hitting the walls with my fist. Finally, I decided to dress for battle. I grabbed a pair of old blue jeans, a red T-shirt, red bandana, and a box cutter.

I had a plan! Since I haven't talked to Spencer in a month, I would call him to pick me up and act like I was not mad at him. I would pretend I enjoyed his rough sex and seduce him into having sex. Once his clothes were off, I would slice him to pieces. In the ghetto, you learn how to use a razor and how to hide razors in your mouth without swallowing them, or between your breasts without getting cut.

My anger was built up from many years of being rejected. I thought I was healed from those feelings, but realized it was dormant, just waiting for the opportunity to show itself. The time had come! All those old feelings were roaring back. All I wanted was to fight back. As I was leaving my bedroom, intent on getting revenge on Spencer, I stopped in front of the mirror to check myself out.

God asked, "Where are you going?"

In disbelief of what I thought I heard, I looked in the mirror. I was angry and said, "Since I'm hurting, I'm going to hurt him."

God said, "Didn't I tell you through my preacher that vengeance is mine." Romans 12:19 states, *"Dearly beloved, avenge not yourself, but rather give place unto wrath: for it is written Vengeance is mine: I will repay, say the lord.* That was what my pastor preached the Sunday prior to the rape. I began to weep because I wanted him to die, but then I turned the box cutter to myself.

I said, "If I can't kill him, then I'll kill myself. I can't live with the thought of being raped, abused, and misused."

In the quiet of my spirit, I heard, "Vengeance is mine. Peace I leave with you; my peace I give to you." I felt a calmness coming over my body. As I walked past my dresser, I accidently knocked over the bible. I turned around to pick it up and noticed that it fell open. As I brought it closer to so I could read it, I noticed the verse John 14:27. It was exactly what was spoken in my spirit, "Vengeance is mine. Peace I leave with you, my peace I give you." It was an unbelievable moment for me! I felt as if God stopped me from making the biggest mistake of my life. I took off my battle clothes with closed eyes and began to weep. I looked in the mirror which again which still reflected my beauty, but my eyes showed pain.

I began to weep, when I felt a hand touch my shoulder. "Are you ok? Why do you have that razor?" It was my mother.

"Yes mom, I'm fine. I'm just tired of life not going the way I planned." Without telling her the real story, I said, "I'm just tired of rejection."

As mothers do, she hugged me and declared, "God is in control of your life and he will work it out for his glory, but for your good." A mother knows her children and knows when they are telling the truth or a lie. I overheard my mom on the phone canceling her appointment, because she knew something was wrong and wanted to stay home with me. She no longer saw Spencer coming to pick me up. When he called the house, I would scream out, "Tell him I am not home." I have not mentioned his name. If my mother asked how Spencer was doing, I would change the subject, because I did not want to speak about the hurt and pain I was going through.

I had to get myself together before going back into the world. I had taken some sick days and vacation days from work, and it was almost over. I isolated myself from the world. I no longer had friends, I called everyone associates. My sisters became my best friends. I only felt comfortable going places with my family. When they didn't have time for me, I would go in a corner to watch television or read a book. I was extremely bitter when my sisters had their boyfriends over. I would always find something negative to say about them, because I was afraid my sisters would experience the same betrayal that I did. My bitterness put a wedge between us.

Nothing seemed the same to me. When people saw love as joy, I saw love as trouble. When girls saw shopping and dressing nice as therapeutic, I saw it as a waste of time.

# RELIEVED BUT GUILTY

I spent the next six months doing the same thing every day: going to work, home, church, and isolating myself from people except for my family. One day while I was waiting on the train to go home from work, I stopped to get a bag of potato chips and a soda at the store that was located on the train station platform. As I sat on the bench waiting for my train, I looked up and saw Spencer's girlfriend, now wife, Kinsley, a few feet away. I tried to pretend not to see her, but it was too late.

"Madelene! Madelene! Where have you been?" Kinsley screamed with excitement while waving her hand frantically back and forth. She had one baby in the stroller and was holding the hand of another child. "I have been trying to call you, but your number was disconnected. I wasn't sure exactly where you lived. And each time I went to your church, you weren't there, or I was told you had just left," she exclaimed.

What Kinsley didn't know, was that I had seen her at church, but I had slipped the other way. I didn't want to talk to her, because I thought she wanted to confront me about Spencer.

Kinsley continued," It was like you dropped off the face of this earth with no contact information."

"I've been busy and staying to myself or with my family because I've changed since we last hung out," I said in a low voice.

Kinsley replied, "Well, I thought you disappeared or were in a depressed because my husband, Spencer, had died in a car accident."

I felt my throat beginning to close and my heart started beating fast as I stuttered and said, "Wh-Wh-What did you say?"

"A few months ago, Spencer died in a car accident." Kinsley repeated. Kinsley proceeded to say, "Spencer and his girlfriend, Mia, were drinking and driving, while I was at home with our children." Kinsley paused while she looked to see if the train was coming. Then she continued, "Where were you when we got married? We had a private ceremony at the beach on Coney Island and knew for sure you were going to be there." Kinsley went on without giving me a chance to respond, "After we got married, Spencer changed. He became aggressive, argumentative, and unstable. Nothing I did anymore was good enough for him. At times, Spencer would seem to change into this person I didn't know, and he would rape me," she said as her voice trailed off.

"Rape, but you are his wife!"

"Wife or not, no means no. Do you know I was scared to leave my children alone with Spencer, because one time I went to the store and when I returned my oldest child was in the corner crying, with bruises on his body. I'm not sure what a three-year-old could have done to make him that mad or cause that many problems in just one hour."

I tried to get a word in, but she just kept on talking.

"One day while he was sleeping, I went through his phone, because I knew he was cheating. I found text messages to three different ladies telling them that he loved them and couldn't wait to be with them again. I woke Spencer up with hot boiling water in my hand, as was getting ready to pour it on him. He pleaded for his life saying that he was going to change. Spencer actually called all his women while I was standing there letting them know that it was over." Kinsley was a person that talked a mile a minute. She continued, "For months, I wouldn't have sex with him, because I wanted to let him know the seriousness of how mistrust can affect a marriage. I made him take every sexual transmitted disease test that was on the market, just to make sure he didn't pass anything to me."

"Wow, you did what? And he actually went and took the tests?"

"Yes, and he began to change. Spencer was coming straight home from work, helped with cooking, cleaning, and spending quality time with me and the kids. Our marriage was getting back on track until a few months ago when he started acting out again. He was coming home late, drinking, being secretive, and demanding sex from me. I refused because he was not acting like my husband; he was not the man I married. The man that was before me was not the man I was familiar with," said Kinsley.

Where is the train? It seems like we've been waiting for quite a while. I looked over her shoulder to see if it was coming, because I really didn't want to hear any more about her life with Spencer, but I didn't want to be rude. When Kinsley saw me looking for the train, she turned to look, also, but there was no train in sight.

Continuing on, Kinsley said, "That night Spencer went out, I asked him not to go because I had a bad feeling that something was going to happen. We argued back and forth until I gave up and said, "I warned you." About one o'clock in the morning, the police came by my house and told me that Spencer had been in an accident and that I needed to go to the local hospital. When I got there, he had already passed away from trauma to his head, just because him and Mia decided it was okay to get a blow job while driving drunk, and they hit a tree. That was the most embarrassing feeling ever! Not only did I know Spencer was cheating, but now, everybody was going to know how he died." With tears in her eyes Kinsley stated," I don't miss him.

I wanted to tell Kinsley the real reason why I quit hanging around them was because Spencer raped me, but this was not the right time. I wanted to tell her how Spencer had attacked me, raped me, and treated me like trash. It was on the tip of my tongue, but before I could say anything, the train came. I felt sorry for Kinsley, but I was glad that Spencer was dead.

Immediately my heart felt the need to repent, because it was not good to rejoice over someone's death, even if they had hurt me.

When I arrived home, I got cleaned up before dinner, walked past the mirror in my bedroom. I was happy, but yet, sad. I felt a weight was lifted off of me. I wasn't ready to be around people, because I still felt overwhelmed. I was relieved that I didn't kill Kinsley, but his lifestyle did. I began to wonder if that is what the Lord meant when he said, "Vengeance is mine." I began to wonder if God told him to repent of his sins before he took that drink, before he cheated on his wife. Although they met at the university, he was a musician in church. I wondered if his pastor had given him a warning before his death. I believe that warnings always come before destruction. Although he raped me, I still cared about his soul.

I felt like my confidence in God and man was taken away from me when I was forced to have sex with my friend. Now all I wanted was to heal. I kept the rape and betrayal to myself for a long time, because of the shame and fear of what my family would say or how they would react towards me. Now, the most important thing for me to do is work on my relationship with God. God does not make mistakes, and he allows things to happen for our good but for his glory. At this point I didn't know what part of rape was for my good, because it left me damaged.

# THE BAD TURNED INTO THE GOOD

In church, I was known to be a very respectful, responsible girl that did not mind helping where help was needed. I went to a church with a lot of relatives. One Sunday, my aunt and uncle approached me to ask if I could baby sit my little cousin, Dana, for several weeks because they were going out of the country and they would pay me. During this time, I was still in college and needed the extra cash, besides I didn't mind helping out. Well, of course I agreed. However, a couple of weeks turned into a couple of months. I became close to Dana. We did a lot of things together. On weekends, we went to the movies, bowling, roller skating, anything we felt like doing. It seemed as if I was spending time with my little sister.

One Friday when Dana got home from school and I got home from work, we had movie night at the house. We popped popcorn, ordered pizza, soda, and wings. we had an open credit card that was left for me to use on anything we needed. We watched a movie called, "A Time to Kill," which told a story about a little black girl getting raped by white men. The father took authority in his own hands by shooting the white boys for raping his daughter. I was not in favor of watching the movie because of my experience, but Dana insisted, so we watched the movie. In the movie the little girl was left in the woods by her brothers and these white boys began to rape her. As she was screaming for her dad to help her, I could feel myself becoming upset. So, I closed my eyes and started praying that Dana wouldn't notice that I was getting upset. My insides were boiling, but I restrained myself. I noticed that Dana was jumpy and had started crying. Maybe this movie was not a good idea for either of us, because it was definitely getting to Dana.

"Dana are you OK?" I asked.

"Why do you want to know? I'm OK," Dana snapped.

"Because you're crying as if you've gone through a similar experience."

Dana looked at me and rolled her eyes. She continued to give me the impression that something was wrong. When the movie showed the little girl crying, Dana mumbled under her breath, "I know how you feel." At one point, she scooted closer to me and asked me to hug her.

"Are OK? Tell me what happened at school. Since you got home, your attitude had changed."

"Nothing is wrong, I just miss my mom."

After the movie was over, Dana asked with a shaky voice, "Could I tell you something?"

"Of course, you can" in a very concerned voice. My ears were opened to anything that Dana had to say.

With tears running down her face, she balled up her fist as if she wanted to punch someone. "Three boys raped me in the back of the staircase at the school. My friend and I were going to class and noticed two senior boys following us, but we thought they were going to class as well. I was a little confused because seniors were not allowed to mingle with freshmen. When they opened the door to the back staircase, there was another boy standing there. He grabbed me and my friend, Amanda, but Amanda got away. Two boys held down my legs, and one of them lifted up my skirt and got on top of me. He penetrated me. It hurt so bad! I screamed, but no one heard me. Each time I made a sound, the boy on top of me would put his hands over my mouth to keep me quiet. I never felt pain like that before. I was a virgin. When the other one tried to get on top of me, they heard a noise and ran. I didn't know what the noise was, only that it scared the boys."

The only thing I knew to do was hold Dana closer and whisper, "I know what it feels like to be raped." It was all too familiar to me. The pain of rape and rage came back to me. Now this child is experiencing the same pain, too. But then, I remembered there were cameras at Dana's school. I said, "Dana, aren't there cameras everywhere in your school? The school should be able to identify those boys. I'm going to call the principal right now."

Dana replied, "No! Wait! I just remembered the back stairway doesn't have a camera.

Just as I was about to ask more questions, Dana got up and started screaming, "My friend Amanda didn't even help me! Amanda didn't even go to get help."

I knew there were some holes in her story, because the security guard at her school walks around every few minutes, and he would have seen those boys. Before I could ask another question, the phone rang telling me that Dana was absent from school. I looked at her with curiosity after listening to her story. I said, "Dana, I know you were not at school today, because those boys would have gotten caught and you probably would have been taken to the hospital. Just to let you know, the phone call I just received was the school secretary informing me that you were not in school. So please don't lie. I want to help you, but you need to tell me the truth. I believe something happened and I do understand your pain."

Dana began to cry and said, "Madelene, please don't be mad at me. I cut school with my friend, Amanda. It was my first-time cutting school. I was curious because everybody was boasting about how much fun these cutting parties are, and I wanted to see for myself. When I got there, it was no fun at all. Everybody was drinking, smoking weed, and having sex everywhere. Even Amanda was hooking up with a guy and left me sitting on the couch alone. I was so scared, because everyone I recognized were seniors and I was just a freshman. Amanda looked at me and told me to loosen up, and she passed me a drink, but I refused. Then Amanda asked her cousin to keep me company while she did her thing."

Dana became choked up as she continued, "Her cousin, Aaron, came to sit with me. At first, he was nice, but then he got rough." She began to cry and said, "Madelene, he hurt me. I told him to stop, but he asked why I came to the party if I didn't want to drink or smoke and have sex. He pulled me to the floor and pulled up my skirt. He hurt me," Dana said.

"Dana, I'm here for you and won't judge you." I looked at her with tears in my eyes, and just held her tight. I wanted to get revenge for her, but I needed to focus on her.

"Madelene, I never felt pain like that, but he wouldn't stop. He kept pushing himself in me until I screamed out loud and told him it hurt. Everyone around us just started saying, 'Yeah man, bust the cherry.' When he was finished raping me, Aaron had the nerve to whisper in my ear to tell me I was no longer a virgin. All I could do was cry. They all just laughed.

I was angry that Dana cut school, but even more angry that she was raped in front of a crowd of people and no one helped. I can't believe that everyone thought what that boy did to her was okay. And the nerve of her friend, Amanda, leaving her alone. I was not going to brush this under the rug. I hugged Dana tight and said, "He will pay for what he did."

Instead of going to sleep we went to the emergency room. I didn't want Dana to suffer in private like I did. As Dana was examined by the doctor, the police came to interview her. She named her abuser, the guys who stood around watching, and her friend, Amanda, who left her alone. I looked at Dana as she was talking to the police and wished I would have had that kind of strength to tell what had happened to me. While Dana was preoccupied with the police and medical staff, I stepped in the hall to contact her parents. I didn't want to interrupt their vacation to give them bad news, but this is something they had to know.

While we waited for my aunt and uncle to return from their vacation, I kept Dana busy by playing games such as Uno, Trouble, Bingo, and other board games. When my uncle and aunt finally came home, they grabbed Dana, embracing her tightly. With tears running down their faces, they promised her they were going to press charges against Aaron for what he had done to her. They, also, told Dana that she was forbidden to speak to Amanda.

As I watched them embrace, it felt good to see that Dana would have the support of her parents while she dealt with this nightmare. But I, also, felt bad because I knew Dana would be scarred for the rest of her life if she didn't get counseling, something I refused to do for myself.

# GIRLS DAY OUT

Since the women's shelter would not be available for a couple of days, I suggested that we needed to have a girl's day out. Besides, I wanted to take Santos shopping for clothes. She, also, needed other essentials as well.

Santos had decided to stay away from her husband until he got help for his anger issues. She knew it was time to stand up for herself. She called her husband on my phone to tell him that she was not coming back because she was tired of getting beat every day. Shirlene and I could hear him yelling and screaming on the phone, "You better bring your ass home or when I find you, I'm going to kill you." The anger and evilness that came through the phone had all of us shaking. Santos began to cry as her husband continuously yelled at her, "Where are you so I can come and get you? Whose phone are you calling from?"

You could tell in her voice that she was scared and didn't know what to say. The fear on her face gave me the impression that she was about to tell him where she was.

"Santos, hang up the phone! You don't have to listen to that type of abuse nor be scared of him," yelled Shirlene.

I said, "Santos, it is time for you to fight for yourself. Fight for your happiness. Fight for your peace. Listen, you think you have had it hard. Let me tell you about this woman in the bible that was bleeding for twelve long years and spent all of her money trying to get healed and nothing worked. When she heard Jesus was coming through town, she said I've had enough of this bleeding. I want to be made whole. As Jesus was walking through town, there was a crowd around him, because they had heard about the miracles he performed. The woman said, "If I could touch the hem of his garment, then I will be made whole." She pushed through the crowd, touched his garment, and she was made whole. I looked Santos straight in the eyes and said, "You have to say, 'Enough is enough' and then, keep pursuing until you see yourself whole."

"Santos looked at me with tears in her eyes and said, "Yes, I have had enough."

I replied "Good, now the journey begins."

We decided to make our way to the spa which was located in the same area as the King's Plaza Mall. We had the deeply relaxing massage therapy which took about an hour. This gave us time to meditate and relax since we were sore after our workout and shopping.

Santos needed to unwind because of all the trauma she has gone through and is still going through. She thanked us for spending time with her. With all the money her husband made, she stated she had never experienced a spa treatment. Shirlene and I decide to go all the way; we took her to get her nails and toes done, and a full makeover. The smile on Santos's face was priceless. I hadn't known her long, but seeing her looking happy, made my soul leap for joy.

After the most exhilarating massage, and getting our nails, toes and face done, I asked Santos what her favorite store was. She was reluctant to accept my generosity, but I told her that since she was going to be with me for two weeks, then she must have clothes to change into. I explained to her that I changed my mind about giving her my clothes, because she deserved to have something new as a metaphor of starting over. After going back and forth trying to convince her to agree to our offer, she finally accepted and told us she loved clothing from New York and Company. "You are the women after my heart, because that is my favorite store. So, we headed there to go shopping." Seeing Santos' eyes light up as we got closer to the store, was like watching a little child at Christmas.

Shirlene whispered to me, "Since you paid for the spa treatment, I want to pay for her clothes."

Once we entered the store, Santos went to the clearance rack first. Shirlene told her she didn't have to buy clothes on the clearance rack, and to be sure to get anything she needed. Santos eyes lit up with so much joy, and she started going back and forth from rack to rack. While she was shopping, Shirlene said, "Santos's husband sounded really scary on the phone. I hope she is done with him for good, because you know how some women are. They say they are done, but the minute their husbands cry and say they're sorry, and that they love them, and bring them flowers, women seem to always walk right back into prison."

"Well, I hope she had enough of getting beat and is ready to move on. God will always provide a way of escape, but it is up to her. If she does go back, at least she was offered some options," I said.

"If she goes back, she may not make it out the next time," Shirlene replied.

"Well, all we can do is pray and show her love. The final decision is hers. She said she was ready to move on, so we'll see."

After shopping until we dropped, we went to Olive Garden to eat. It was so good. We were all talking and laughing, and enjoying our meal, when Santos asked, "How did y'all get so happy?"

"I was not always in a happy place. I went through a lot of hurt, pain, disappointment, and rejection before I became the person you see. I want you to know that behind every smile there is a story."

Santos said, "But Madelene you are outgoing and bold."

I laughed and said, "Let me finish telling you about me. I almost allowed silence to kill me."

# SILENCE IS A KILLER

After the rape of my little cousin, I was still trying to self-heal from my own abuse. I went to many revivals at church. I talked about my abuse to others, but never revealed that I was a victim, because of the embarrassment. When I thought I was ready to tell people that I was a victim, my throat would seem to close up, and my face would break out into a sweat. I realized that it was not the right time, and I didn't feel safe enough to tell my story. I was not the type of person to let people feel sorry for me, or to try to fix me, or try to appease me to make it all better, because it would not feel real.

The problem with being silent is that it started to hinder my relationships with everyone. Silence can stink, silence can also kill your character, silence can kill you. Have you ever had gas in your stomach, and when you begin to pass the gas, it was loud? You thought that it was going to smell up the room, but in fact it was just loud and embarrassing with no smell. On the other hand, when you have gas, again you try to hold it in, but can't. This time, it is quiet and long, and smells so strong. In fact, the smell is so awful, it will clear the room. People may even say things like, "What died in you?" That is just an example of how the silence of not telling someone about my abuse was affecting me. I was stinking up the room with my negativity; nothing was ever good in my eyes. I was crying for help on the inside, but no one recognized that my silence was killing me, because my appearance seemed so strong. There were so many negative thoughts about people and relationships going on in my mind, preventing me from being healed. The problem is that no one knew I was suffering in silence. I knew this was not good, because I started secluding myself from people and walking around putting on a façade of being happy. I just couldn't bring myself to talk about what happened.

One day my sister confided in me about her relationship with her boyfriend. She believed he was cheating, but she didn't have proof. He would lie about where he had been and would come home smelling like perfume. When his phone rang, he turned it face down when they were at the table so she wouldn't see who was calling him. My response was just leave him. It came out so mean and forceful that my sister said, "Wow! If I didn't know any better, I would have thought he was cheating on you."

I said," I'm sorry! I just don't want you hurt like I've been."

When my sisters and I would go out to eat, or go out for a day of fun, if a guy was paying one of them attention, I would act impatient and irritated, causing a scene so we could leave. I became overprotective of my sisters. I wanted to know where they were at all times, and when they got home. I questioned them like I was interrogating them. They didn't tell me anything, because they felt I was too controlling. My sisters told me that I needed to get some friends. Apparently, they didn't know how I really felt about people at this point in my life. I didn't know how to have a good time without fear and doubt overtaking me.

It was Thanksgiving and my mom had cooked the most amazing meal. We had macaroni and cheese, collard greens with smoked neck bones, field peas & snap with ham hocks, steamed cabbage, potato salad, white rice, yellow rice, cornbread, turkey, ham, fried chicken, and plenty of pies, and cakes. The kitchen was full of food and smelled like a soul food restaurant. There was no place to sit at the table, so we made our living room into a dining room for this special occasion. The food was so good.

I was glad my cousins had come over to eat dinner with us, because I didn't feel alone since everyone had a guest, except me. After dinner we played Uno, Trouble, and Monopoly. We were up late having family fun. The laughter that was in the air made me forgot about what was going on inside of me.

The day after Thanksgiving, my family was watching TV when someone knocked on the door. It was my sister's boyfriend. I thought to myself, *"He was just here yesterday. Why is he here again today?"* He took a seat near me. When my sister left the room, I looked at him and said, "If you hurt my sister, I will hurt you." I know he felt the evilness in my eyes as I stared hard at him without blinking. "If I think you are hurting her, I will get my brothers to handle you." My sister called him into the kitchen. As he stood up to leave, I said, "Bye, enjoy the food, but don't forget what I said." My heart was satisfied, because I felt like I had intimidated this guy. The power of thinking I was in control was a strange, but good feeling.

# NOT AGAIN

A few months later, I was approached by a young man in the library at the university. He said "Hi, my name is William." The look on my face should have let him know that I was not interested, but he went on to say, "You're Madelene, right?"

"Why do you want to know? "I replied.

William said," Because I noticed you across the room during our Christian Club meeting, and thought you are the most beautiful woman I've ever seen."

"Listen, William, that is your name, right?"

"Yes," he said.

"Well, I am not interested in whatever game you are trying to play, besides there are plenty of pretty women in this school. Pick one to approach and leave me alone. Thank you and have a blessed day," I said as I turned and walked away.

He seemed so determined to get to know me. Everywhere I went, I noticed William. I purposely tried to avoid him, but he always seemed to be following me. When he approached me in public, he would smile and say, "Hello Madelene." I brushed him off by rolling my eyes and walking in another direction, hoping he got the hint.

William was not present at one of our Christian Club group meetings. So, I thought it was the perfect time to invite everyone to my church to fellowship with me, besides it was my Sunday to sing in the choir. They agreed and looked forward to worshipping with me at my church.

Sunday finally came, and I was looking in the congregation to see if my Christian group had shown up. To my surprise, there was William. Before the pastor delivered his sermon, my choir sang a song by Rev. Timothy Wright called, "Trouble Don't Last Always." It seemed like everyone, including me, was in the glory of worship. Nothing else mattered at the moment, but me and God. I was so honest to God, letting him know that I had been hurting for a long time and wanted to be healed. I was jumping and praising Him when a mother in the church named Mother Houston whispered in my ear that I was going to be ok, as if she knew something was wrong. It felt so good to worship God freely. The pastor preached a great sermon. I looked over at my Christian group and saw that William was praising God, too. I immediately thought, *"Why is he playing with God to try to impress me?"*

After church William came over to me and said, "WOW! the worship experience here was awesome! I felt as if God answered my prayer."

"Good for you," I said with a smile as I walked away.

William grabbed my arm, but I quickly snatched my arm away.

"Don't ever grab my arm like that again!" I said firmly as I stared him straight in his face.

"I apologize. Listen I know you told me to leave you alone, but if you can reconsider, I would love to take you out to dinner one night," William said. The expression on my face must have made him uncomfortable, because he immediately said, "But no pressure, I just want to get to know you."

"Listen, I'm not the one you are looking for, please find someone else," I murmured.

"Ok, maybe next time," William said with a smile.

During every Christian society meeting at the university, William would walk over to me and say, "Hello." I would just wave and keep walking. We had meetings twice a week to plan a street ministry. We had come up with the idea of giving out bible tracks to everyone in the street that would accept it. We had to work in groups of six for safety reasons to do evangelism. William made sure he was part of my group. While we were supposed to be evangelizing, William seemed distracted because he was constantly watching me. He could not keep his eyes off of me. He was so persistent. Finally, he said, "Excuse me, Madelene. Where do you work? I would love to take you out to lunch."

"William, I told you so many times that I am not interested in dating right now. So again, can you flirt with someone else?"

William looked at me and said, "Okay, maybe next time." He had been turned down so many times by me that you would think he would have given up. However, my rejection didn't seem to phase him at all, as a matter of fact it seemed like he enjoyed the chase. He was acting like Steve Urkel from the sitcom, "Family Matters," where Steve would ask Laura on a date, but she would always say no. That didn't stop Steve. He knew one day her "no" would eventually turn into "yes."

A couple of days later after our group meeting, our mutual friend, Tommy, told me he could vouch for William. He said Tommy was a great guy that really loves God, has a desire to see people saved, as I did. He, also, said, "Tommy wants to get to know me. In fact, you guys have a lot in common." Tommy was so convincing, that I finally agreed to go on a date with William.

The following Friday night we went on our first date. I thought it was going to be a waste of his and my time, because I had no desire to date anyone at that point in my life. Although I was anxious to get out of the house, I wasn't that excited to go out with William. I didn't feel prepared mentally to date.

I heard a car pull up, so I looked out the window and saw William's car. I thought he was going to blow the horn for me to come downstairs, but to my surprise, he got out of the car and proceeded to walk towards my building. I thought to myself, *Hmmm, very impressive*. There was a knock on the door, and I was glad no one was home, because I didn't want anyone to meet him. I yelled, "I'm coming." When I opened the door, there stood a very handsome tall, dark-skinned man with all black on and he was looking good.

"Are you ready to go?" he said."

"Sure." I grabbed my purse and walked toward the door.

"You look nice," said William.

"Really?" I asked sarcastically.

William was the perfect gentleman. He opened the door for me, he asked, "Are you comfortable, because you are holding your pocketbook tightly as if someone was going to steal it from you?"

I chuckled, "Well, I am a little uncomfortable, because I have not been on a date in a longtime and I'm not sure if I am ready for this."

"Well, I promise to make sure you will have a good time," said William.

I still felt insecure and didn't trust him.

William asked, "Is there any particular place you wanted to eat?"

"No, I'm not picky."

William had the night planned out for us. it started out with a dinner at a restaurant called BBQ's in Manhattan. Sitting at the table was awkward for me, because I had nothing to talk about. I was not going to talk about my life; I made that loud and clear. I told him if he wanted to have sex with me, then I was not the one, because I was waiting until I got married, and furthermore, there was more to life than sex. William said that's not what he wanted from me. He said he really liked me. He was very talkative and seemed very goal oriented. He wanted to know about my future plans and goals for my life. No one had ever taken an interest in my dreams and goals. So, I was beginning to loosen up and enjoyed the conversation. We talked for hours.

After dinner, William didn't want the night to end. So, he asked if we could drive over to the promenade in Brooklyn. I must have really enjoyed his company, because I agreed. As we were driving, he started telling me how beautiful I was and that he was attracted to me. Not knowing where he was going with this conversation, I grabbed my bag tight, and looked at him with a *"Don't get any ideas"* kind of look." He continued talking, and I realized he was just being nice. When we got to Brooklyn Heights, we walked through the promenade. We found an empty bench and looked out over the water at the lights in Manhattan and on the bridge. This was my first time here, and it was breath taking. He sat close to me and asked, "Can I put my arms around you?"

"No, I'm good," I said firmly.

We sat there for hours talking, laughing, connecting, and discovering that we had a lot in common. Finally, the night was coming to an end, and I was ready to go home. The drive home was fun and relaxing. He was the perfect gentleman, although I thought he was going to try to kiss me, but he didn't. I didn't want him to, but it was just a thought. When we got to my apartment building, he walked me upstairs and asked, "Can I see you again?"

"Well, I really enjoyed your company. You made me feel special. So, I don't mind if we see each other again," I said as I opened the door to my apartment. I felt him looking at me as he pressed the elevator button. He was really into me! This night was perfect.

There was not a day that went by without us calling each other. We spent time together every weekend going out to eat or doing other activities, such as bowling, roller skating, or going to amusement parks. However, the promenade was our special place to enjoy the view and conversation. After about the tenth time going to the promenade, I finally let him put his arms around me. William told me this is how he liked to hold his woman, and that one day he will propose to a special lady right here in this spot.

I was starting to come alive and experience being happy, again. Even my family started to notice a difference. I didn't act bitter or argumentative anymore. They were wondering what was going on and whether or not I was seeing someone. But I kept him a secret, because I was not ready to introduce him to the family, because I wanted to make sure he was sincere about our friendship. In my mind if you introduce your boyfriend to your family, then the relationship is serious.

We were beginning to connect on a spiritual level. I made it clear that I was not going to have sex with him. At least that was what my mouth said, but for the first time my body was saying something different each time we got together. I was actually falling in love but could not believe it. I still was not completely healed or delivered, because I was holding on to the memories and anger I felt because of the rape and abuse. Although William made my life with him easy, I still knew my pain from the abuse was still present in my life. One day when we were together, William looked in my eyes and asked, "Why are you so secretive and mean? I'm not here to hurt you, only to show you love."

I took a deep breath and explained, "William, it is not that I am secretive. I'm not sure of your motive. In the beginning I didn't want anything to do with you. Even though I turned you down numerous times, here you are, still wanting to be with me."

He said "I will not hurt you. If I do, then I would be hurting Jesus, and that is not what I'm about. Listen, I want my life to please God and my family." I knew he came from a very successful family filled with doctors, lawyers, preachers, teachers, accountants and entrepreneurs. I didn't want to get too deeply involved, because I wasn't sure if I was ready, yet, I was falling in love with him, and I was scared.

Gradually, he began to break down the walls I had put up. I finally started feeling safe again. Having someone take the time to spend with me, and get to know me, to step in and be my hero, was like a breath of fresh air which caused me to just inhale slowly, then exhale. I could not believe that I was giving someone a chance to be my close friend. Regardless, I kept my word and commitment to God regarding my body; I kept myself pure at the time.

I was enjoying the time I spent with William, my new friend, who I now, officially called my boyfriend. I continued to camouflage what was on the inside of me, the pain of the not knowing his real purpose, and still wondering if he was going to do the same thing that Spencer had done. It is funny how people can function, but yet be dysfunctional. Each time William tried to kiss me, it triggered a memory of Spencer. I would make an excuse not to kiss him, or to be intimate with him. I would always say I'm waiting to get married, but in fact I was just not in that state of mind, not even for a kiss.

William took me everywhere he went. He expressed to me that I was his rib, and he could not go anywhere without his rib. He was not ashamed of me. We attended church together, social gatherings, and couples' dates with his friends. He seemed to be proud to have me by his side. I was beginning to like, or perhaps, love him more and more. It seemed like he was helping me close my wounds.

As the months went by, we spent more time together. One day, we went to a private park in New Jersey that was recommended and set up by his boss. William had a blanket, a picnic basket with hero sandwiches, fruit, potato chips, and wine. He laid out the blanket and asked me to have a seat. He sat next to me and placed our lunch on a silver platter. He talked about his future goals and dreams again as we were eating and drinking. It was so refreshing, just listening to what was on his heart. He turned on his small radio so we could listen to music. Luther Vandross's song, "One Night with You," came on. William stood up, reached for my hand, and said, "Would you like to dance? I smiled and stood up. We began to slow dance. William looked in my eyes and said, "I'm falling in love with you."

Hearing the word love, almost made me let my guard down. For a moment, I almost forget about my commitment to God, not to have sex. William seemed to have taken possession of my heart and mind. I took a deep breath and said, "I love you too," as tears trickled down my face.

"Don't worry, I got you," he said.

"Thank you, and I got you too," I said as I exhaled. Maybe now I can finally live. We had a long passionate kiss that sparked fireworks in my heart and hormones began raging through my body. I had to maintain self-control, even when he couldn't. Although it was difficult, I still stayed strong.

After we professed our love for each other, we decided it was time for us to meet each other's family. Our parents knew about us, but we had never met each other's family, because I was not ready. First, I arranged dinner with my family because they're very loving, down to earth, fun, and compassionate.

The day finally came, and my family was excited to meet William. They knew he must be special to me, because I had not invited anyone to our home in a very long time. He knocked on the door. My heart started pounding out my chest as I opened the door. He looked so handsome that I began to feel warm on the inside. I introduced him to everyone. They treated him like they had known him for a long time. Once dinner was over, my brothers invited him into the other room for a big brother talk. My sister kept reiterating how handsome William was and that we looked good together. She asked if we were planning to get married, because she said he looks at me as if he was truly in love. I just smiled and said, "Thank you! We'll see.

The evening went well. William seemed to love my family. He was especially impressed with the fact that we lived in the projects, but didn't have the mentality of gang bangers, welfare check recipients, or being lazy, or any of those stereotypes. I reminded him that many famous people lived in the projects, like Sean Corey Carter, known professionally as Jay-Z, who is a rapper, songwriter, producer and a rich businessman, and Justice Sonia Sotomayor, who is the first Latina to become a US Supreme Court Justice. No one can help where they have to live to make ends meet, but they can contribute to molding their future by hard work and staying focused.

My family was a goal-setting family that did not take "No" for an answer. It did not matter how long it took to reach our goals; we knew our goals would come to pass through faith. William seemed to enjoy spending time getting to know my family. I felt so close to him, and really felt in my heart that he meant every word when he said he would not hurt me.

Later, I walked him to his car, and he asked if I wanted to go for a ride. Of course, we ended up at the promenade. We kissed and talked and talked and kissed. This time, I was not strong enough to say no. This was the first time in my life that my heart and body felt loved, and wanted to be loved, because I was in love. My hormones began to rage as we began to kiss again. He wrapped me tightly in his arms and slowly moved his hands up and down my back. After kissing my lips, he began to kiss my neck, which gave me a good sensation moving through my body.

He looked at me and said in a caring voice, "I want you to know that I don't just want sex from you, because that's considered casual sex. Madelene, what I want is to make love to you, because the love we have for each other is genuine. I know you wanted to wait until you're married, or until "we're" married he smiled. Can I please make love to you?

I said, "Yes! I'm ready."

He asked, "Are you sure? I don't want to rush you. I love you and don't want anything to stop you from loving me."

I took a deep breath and said, "Yes! Yes!"

It was eight o'clock in the evening. We went to the hotel that was a block over from where we were. I had a lot going on in my mind, wondering whether this was the right thing to do. I had made a vow to God and didn't want to break it. I was scared I would have a flashback from being raped by Spencer and cause a scene. So much was going through my head as William held my hand as we walked into the hotel.

When we got into the hotel room, we talked about marriage, how he saw me as his wife, and where we were going to live. He expressed that he knew I had made a vow to God, and he wanted me to keep it; ye, he also wanted to make love to me. I wanted to make love to him, too, but I was so scared of being hurt and disappointed in him as well as myself. However, that evening was so special. He took his time and showed me how it felt to make love to someone you love. I have never ever felt the power of love like that before. When we were finished, I cried like a baby for two reasons. One was because I failed God, and the other was because I was truly in love.

Now it was my turn to meet his family. I was extremely nervous, because I had never been invited to dinner by someone I was dating and in love with. I went to get my hair, nails, and toes done. Afterwards, I went to buy a new outfit, because I really wanted to impress his family. Once I got home, I took a long shower. Then, I put perfume on and did my make up just right. As I looked in the mirror, I became shaky with fears of not wanting to get hurt again, but it was too late for that, because I had already given him my body.

I slowly put on my beautiful yellow sun dress with my royal blue accessories, yellow and royal blue belt, with royal blue high heel sandal shoes. I thought I was stunning. My family also commented on how beautiful I looked. William knocked on my door. He had on blue jeans with a nice yellow polo shirt, since we had planned to dress in the same colors. When he saw me, his eyes opened wide as if he saw Cinderella before him. He looked at me and said, "You are very beautiful." A smile spread across my face. William spoke to my family, then, grabbed my hands gently and looked in my eyes and said, "Are you ready?" It was supposed to be a 30-minute ride to his home, but it seemed like an eternity. Our conversation was very stimulating and hopeful. He kept telling me how he could see a future with me and would make that happen one day. It seemed like he really wanted to marry me some day, because he again asked me where I wanted to live and other futuristic questions. It seemed like he was preparing to move out of town once we graduated from college and wanted me to go with him.

The big moment came as we drove up to his house. My first impression was, "Wow, this is beautiful." He looked at me and asked, "Are you ready?"

Joking, I responded, "No, but let's go in."

William opened the door, and I saw a high ceiling, beautiful cream colors on the wall, tall windows, hardwood floors that were glowing, and a beautifully decorated dining room table that seated at least twenty people. His father sat at the head of the table and his three brothers, two sisters, and their guests sat on the side. They all smiled and greeted us. His mother came in and sat in her chair at the other end of the table, opposite her husband.

I whispered to William, "Are we late? Everyone is already seated at the table."

"No, I timed it just right. I wanted us to be fashionably late so all eyes would be on you." Looking around the table, he continued, "Hello, family. This is my girlfriend, Madelene. Madelene, this is my family."

"It's a pleasure to finally meet you. We've heard some wonderful things about you," said Mr. Robert.

"It's a pleasure to meet you all," I smiled.

"Please have a seat," said his mother, Mrs. Clara, as she looked me up and down. William pulled out my chair; we sat down.

William's siblings began to say, "Hi, welcome to the family."

Mr. Robert said, "Let's hold hands to pray." We grasped each other's hands, and his father began to pray. He prayed in a very deep, authoritative voice that gave me chills. When he finished, we all said, "Amen."

Soon after, the questions started, *"Where do you live? Who are your parents? Where do they work? What are your future plans?"* I felt like I was being interrogated. I was so nervous that when I tried to answer their questions, it was as if my tongue was tied. I sounded like the teacher in a Charlie Brown movie. I was so embarrassed, that I sat quiet for the rest of the evening.

The environment was very different from what I was used to. I watched as they were in sync passing the food and neatly putting it on their plate. Dinner was delicious. The evening was nice, professional, and interesting. After dinner, we went in the den to watch television. There was no laughter, just upscale, formal, and boring conversation. I thought to myself. This family needs to loosen up. They act like they're at a church banquet, or at a presidential dinner party.

Finally, William asked, "Ready to go?"

I jumped up so fast from the couch and said, "Yes, I do have to get back." We said our goodbyes to the family.

On the drive back, William asked, "How did you enjoy the evening?"

"It was great," but in the back of my mind I thought it was boring. When we arrived at my home, he walked me up to my apartment. We gazed longingly into each other's eyes. I smiled and gently kissed him and said, "Goodnight."

That night, the overwhelming feeling of love filled my heart. I felt alive! Maybe, I can finally move on from my negative past.

Every day that William and I spent time together, was helping to build my trust in people and relationships again. William always saw the good things in people and situations. He was so gentle, positive, and handsome. He told me he loved me. I even expected him to hold my hand while we walked down the streets. When we had a date in the park, he held me tight while we swayed to music. Dancing was our special moment of intimacy. It was just perfect, and he was my hero. I prayed to God, thanking Him for someone who loved me in spite of the fact that I was still broken.

# THE REJECTION

We dated for two years and were getting ready to graduate. I started noticing how funny he began to act towards me. He stopped taking me out every weekend, started ignoring me, and rejected my calls. When we were together, he was distant, and seemed sad. He could not look me in the eyes." What's wrong?" I asked.

"I truly love you, but," his voice sounded strained and trailed off before he finished.

"But what?" I responded.

William never explained his behavior. It was like we were beginning to switch roles; He seemed broken, and I was heading toward becoming whole. I knew something was not right.

One day, William took me to a beautiful restaurant called Tavern on the Green in Central Park. He had made the reservations and asked to sit by the window. As we waited to be seated, he looked at me and smiled. He told me how beautiful I was and that he loved the smell of my perfume. William had helped me get to a better place within myself. We were graduating from college next week. He had a job offer at a law firm as an intern. Although I was still a bank teller, I had aspirations of moving up in the banking industry.

I glanced around the restaurant. This place is breath taking. It looked like a glass palace and you could tell it was very pricey. William always took me to the nicest restaurants and treated me so special. I felt so comfortable about our relationship, that I began talking about marriage. Since he had told me he loved me, I had broken my commitment to God because of him. I was okay with it I was so excited, because I really thought he was the one, my future husband, my king. With a big smile on my face, I said, "William, when we get married, I want to move out of New York to New Jersey to the suburbs to fulfill the American dream of living in a house with a white picket fence, but no dog."

William looked me in the face and said sternly, "God didn't tell me that you were going to be my wife!"

I stopped in my tracks and leaned closer towards him to make sure I had heard him correctly and said, "What? Can you repeat yourself?"

With his eyebrow raised, he looked me in my eyes and said a bit louder, "God didn't tell me that *you* were going to be my wife!"

William's words hit me as hard as a hollow point bullet. BOOM! His words were piercing and penetrating my arteries. He made sure that it pierced my heart, making sure I would never love again. My heart was finished! Mortal Kombat style.

The trigger had been pulled! I felt paralyzed, unable to breathe, unable to move. The room was loud, but I couldn't make out what was being said. Everything moved in slow motion. My heart was beating fast and tears began to fill my eyes. I stared at him in disbelief!

Pulling the trigger again, this time aiming to end me, killing all hope within me, he looked at me and said, "In fact, I brought you here so you could enjoy our last night together, because I have to break up with you. You don't fit into my family."

My face suddenly felt contorted as I glared at him. I grabbed my glass of wine and threw it all over him and stormed out of the restaurant, leaving the sweet fragrance of my perfume floating in the air. As I exited the beautiful restaurant, I realized I lived too far to walk to my apartment in my heels. It was too late to take the train. While I stood outside trying to figure out what to do, questions filled my head. Why did I believe his lies? How could I let this happen again? What is up with men? Why did I let him in my heart? I felt terrible knowing I had broken my commitment to God by making love to him. He had told me that if he hurt me, he would be hurting God. Well, I guess God is crying his eyes out, too, because my heart is breaking in a million pieces.

Suddenly, I heard William calling my name, "Madelene!" I turned around to see him coming towards me, looking disheveled from the wine I had poured on him, leaving his clothes, wet and stained. He looked a mess. As he approached me, he said, "Madelene, let me talk to you."

With tears in my eyes, I said angrily, "You have nothing to say to me! I trusted you. I gave you my heart. I gave you my body. You told me you loved me and acted like you wanted to marry me. Why did you come in my life just to break my heart in pieces? You said you would never hurt me."

William grabbed me and said, "It's not my intention to hurt you. I do love you, and want to be with you, but I can't."

I pointed my finger in his face and shouted, "You can't, or you won't?" I put my hands on my hips as I paced angrily back and forth in front of him.

Williams said, "Please, let me take you home."

At first, I was going to refuse, but I got in the car because I had no other way to get home.

William said, "Please don't be angry!

"Oh, angry is not the choice word I would use to describe my feelings right now. I'm furious!" I said through clenched teeth.

"I'm sorry, Madelene. I do love you, he said."

I interrupted him and said, "If you love me, then tell me what is going on? What is this sudden change? Your behavior does not make any since." William looked at me, tears slowly streamed down his face. He opened his mouth to speak, but shook his head, and didn't say anything else the rest of the way to my house. Being the gentleman that he was, he opened the car door, walked me to my door, and turned to walk away without uttering a word.

I needed an explanation of what had just taken place. I was numb. William's words replayed in my head as if I pressed rewind and action! Too bad I could not cut and edit that moment. Depression knocked at my door, entered it, and took over. Numbness, anxiety, and embarrassment were my scars. No cream or bandages could cover these gashes he left. The feeling of rejection came back ten times harder. I pondered to myself how I was not going to let anyone hurt me again.

As much as I tried not to think about William, I was still trying to figure out what happened to our relationship. Over the past few years of dating him, I had gotten to know one of his sisters, Bethany. I took a chance and called her and explained that William had broken up with me.

Bethany said, "My brother loves you very much, and my dad adores you. I think you were the perfect fit, but our mom and my other brothers and sisters were giving him a hard time. My mom told him if he continued in the relationship with you, he would get cut out of the will. She was fine when he was in school sowing his oats, but now, she said he has to find a better fit for the family. You see, our mom is the one in control of the family, and whatever she says goes."

I thought about the times I was at Williams' house. There were several times a young lady was at their house during dinner at the same time I was there. I noticed William would eat quickly and want to leave as soon as he finished. He always seemed upset when she was around. When I asked who the young lady was that I had never been introduced to, he would always say she was his mother's friend. One evening, it was just her and I in the den, because Mrs. Clara and William had gone to the kitchen to prepare our meal. I took advantage of this opportunity to talk to this girl. "Hey Lady, I've noticed that you come to several family dinners, but no one has introduced you to me. I'm Madelene, William's girlfriend, and you are?"

She smirked, "I'm Gloria, a friend of the family."

Before I could ask another question, William called me to the table to eat. I said, "Gloria, well, I guess it was a pleasure to finally meet you."

"Same here," she said.

Once I had a seat at the table, I asked William, "Why haven't you introduced me to Gloria?"

"Because she is not important. She's my mother's friend, not mine. Besides, you are the only woman I am concerned about."

But my gut told me that something was not right. Although William never treated me differently in front of the family or this young lady, I knew something was up, because one evening I heard his mom in the kitchen saying, "She does not fit in this family and will not be anything in life." I didn't know who she was referring to, but I felt that the "she" his mother was talking about was me.

Bethany went on to say, "On top of that, my mother called you a project girl, whose parents raise you with a project mentality. She said your life will amount to nothing. She told William, "You can take her out of the projects, but you can't take the project out of her." Bethany went on to say, "Madelene, I think you are a beautiful young lady. When my brother is around you, he is so happy and focused. He included you in all of our family plans. It's just my mother who has the problem. She's giving him an extremely hard time." Pulling the phone from my ears in disbelief of what I just heard I replied, "Well, if he is not strong enough to fight for our love against your mother, maybe this is for the best."

I thanked Bethany for being honest with me and hung up the phone. My heart seemed to be pounding in pain. I was furious that his mother judged me based on where I lived, because I came from the most loving, decent family there was. I can't help where I was born, but I can help where I am going.

From that point on in my life, it seemed like rejection was all I was faced with. When I applied for positions, I was rejected for jobs I thought I was qualified for. I was rejected for different positions in my alumni Christian society club. I was rejected for positions that I wanted in my church. I was not sure what was going on. Everywhere I turned, there was a "NO." It seemed like

"Rejection" was written on my face. Finally, I had enough of rejection, and became bitter. Now, I just wanted to get even.

I felt like God had let me down, because he allowed me to love again, only to get hurt. I started dating anyone with a penis, but I didn't sleep with all of them. My dresses got shorter, pants got tighter, and my breast were showing. I was out to hurt anyone who liked me. So many guys found me attractive. I would say things to make them feel special so they would think they were the only one in my life. In fact, I learned how to juggle multiple men at a time. I was so good at it, that I learned to break up with them in the winter, so I didn't have to buy them Christmas gifts, but I always managed to receive gifts. I showed attention to them after Valentine's Day, because I didn't want to spend time with just one. As I dated these men, they fell in love with me; not knowing my only intention was to hurt them like I had been hurt.

During those times, I was not myself. I began to meet a lot of new people outside the church, people who partied every weekend. I enjoyed the party life. The only person who knew the truth about me being a church girl, was a girl named Alayah who I had met at church. She was never a consistent member. When she was in trouble, she would come to church for prayer in hopes that God would help her. Once her troubles were over, she would become an occasional church member again.

When we went to the club and hit the dance floor, we would dance all night. I was a very good dancer. One night, Alayah and I put a guy in a sandwich, and danced the night away. I was really out of control to the point where my mom didn't recognize me anymore. I would come home when I thought everyone was asleep. Then, I would get up early and leave before anyone woke up. I even slowed down going to church because I stayed out too late.

Whenever my mom saw me, she would always say, "I'm praying for you and whatever happened to William." My mother was very observant and was aware of the changes taking place in my life. She looked me in the eyes and said, "Never live for men or any person, because people will fail you every time and they will cause your life to go up and down like a roller coastal. But if you live for God, who is always constant, always there, He will never fail you." One night when I got home extremely late, I heard her in the living room praying for all her children. I walked in right when she called my name. She said, "Lord, whoever hurt my child, Madelene, please mend her heart. Turn her around and place her back at your feet." I took a shower and got in the bed. A couple of minutes later, she was anointing my head and my young siblings' heads with oil. By this time, my older siblings had already left the house. They were married and working on their careers. Now, I was the oldest in the home. As she laid hands on me and said, "Lord, cover her under your blood as she goes in and out of places," my mother made the sign of a cross on my head. After she did that, I closed my eyes and fell fast asleep.

The following Saturday night, Alayah and I decided to drive to Atlantic City to a reggae club we had heard about. While we were waiting to go inside Club J, Alayah said," Madelene, someone just called your name, except they said "Evangelist Madelene." I looked around but didn't see anyone I knew. How could that be? This was our first time at this hole in the wall club in Atlantic City. No one should have known us in this place. Plus, why would they add a title like evangelist to my name? Alayah asked me again, "Madelene who knows you?"

I said, "No one, stop tripping."

Minutes later, Alayah looked at me said, "Someone here is calling your name again, saying 'Madelene the Evangelist.'" We scanned the crowd again but saw no one we knew.

"They can't be calling my name, because no one knows me, and why would they say Evangelist. Girl, I think that's the Hennessey you drank earlier talking to you."

"Let's go!" Alayah said. "This is scaring me, because I do hear someone calling your name. The last time they called your name so loud they have me shaking, and you're telling me you didn't hear it? We need to leave right now."

After leaving the club, I dropped Alayah off. While I was driving home, I heard a small, still voice saying, *I didn't call you to party. I called you to serve me.* Looking around, shocked, I immediately began to repent. I had to find my way back to God. I knew it was because of my mother's prayer to God concerning me several nights ago that had me hearing the voice of God. There's nothing like a praying mother to help get you back on track.

One Friday night I went to a football game with my sisters. I had on my new drop-dead gorgeous outfit. It was a pink Adidas jumpsuit that accentuated my figure, along with matching sneakers. I definitely demanded attention in that outfit. I spotted the love of my life, William, with his new fiancé, and yes, it was the girl from the dinner. Surprisingly, I felt nothing. William walked his fiancé to their seats, but soon found his way back to me, with a look of guilt. "Madelene, I need to apologize for how I treated you. I really was madly in love with you. I wanted to marry…"

Before he could finish, I looked at him through squinted eyes, raised my left eyebrow and said, "God didn't tell me you were going to be my husband. Besides, God is finished crying and so am I." I looked him up and down and skipped away like a little girl who just got a new toy. That was the best payback I could have given him for the pain he put me through, the abandonment, rejection, and low self-esteem I felt, because of his mother's control issues. I thought to myself, *if pleasing other people make you happy, then that is you; but being silent about your true feelings will kill you and I know all too well about how silence can kill.*

# PRINCE CHARMING

As time passed, I was finally in a happy place. I still was not stable enough financially, because I could not find a decent paying job. Being a bank teller does not pay well, and at that time there were no available positions to move up, even with a bachelor's degree. I did not give up, because I knew my day was coming. I understood the saying, "You have to crawl before you walk," and "Be patient." At this point, I just wanted to work on my complete self, the total mind, body, and soul. I went to the gym to work on my body, enrolled in leadership classes at church, and began to develop a strong relationship with God.

After a long day at the gym, I was running to catch the train. There was a gentleman running beside me to catch the same train. We laughed because even though we were running and pushing people out the way, we still missed the train. He looked at me with stars in his eyes, and introduced himself, "Hi, I'm Corey."

I was very reluctant to give my real name, but I thought to myself it wouldn't matter, because we probably won't see each other again, anyway. "I'm Madelene.

"It's a pleasure to meet you," he responded.

"Likewise," I said. Since the next train wasn't scheduled to arrive for another thirty minutes, we sat down, and he talked. He began to tell me his whole life story and how he was looking for someone to love him for him, and not what he had in the bank. At that point, I ignored him because I was not the one. After several minutes of him talking about himself, he said, "Tell me about yourself."

I was very brief. "I am a church girl, and you'll find me there. I go to Spirit and Truth. That's all I have to say."

"Is there anything else?" he said looking at me curiously.

"No!" I replied firmly. I was not interested in him or hearing what he had so say, because I just knew we were not going to see each other again.

"Well, can I have your telephone number?"

"Sure," I answered, and gave him the church's phone number.

Months had gone by since that brief encounter with Corey. One Sunday after service, I noticed a gentleman sitting in the back of the church wearing a country-looking suit. It was a long red suit jacket with red pants, white shirt, red tie, and red shoes. He looked like a pimp. He was very noticeable and appeared out of place.

After service he came up to me with the brightest smile and said, "Hello, Madelene."

"Do I know you?"

"Yes, we met at the train station a few months ago. It took me a longtime to find this church, because you left me with no details and a number that no one answers," he stated.

"Yes, of course. I remember you," I said.

"Can I take you out to eat? he asked.

"Yes, where do you want to meet?" I responded. At this point in my life, I was comfortable with myself. I knew to meet in a public place, have my own money, and drive myself to meet my date. I was no longer afraid of dating, and didn't mind meeting new people, but nothing serious. Relationships just didn't seem to work for me. Besides, I was focusing on getting myself in order.

On our first date, I enjoyed everything about him. That surprised me, because I still felt bitter about my past because of what I had been through, but I was doing better at coping. However, I was not ready to have a close relationship with a guy again, but I didn't have a problem with being friends. I noticed that every time I decided to serve God, and now I was even exploring evangelism, a leech (man) would come along to suck the blood right out of me, trying to distance me from pursuing greatness in my life.

Corey and I had been dating for about six months before he became very persistent about being with me exclusively. He treated acted like our relationship was on a very serious level.

He was someone I wanted to marry, because he was funny, respectful, and appeared to be truthful. As time went by, I met his family. His family environment was warm and loving. It almost felt like I was at home with my family. His mother was very motherly and caring towards me. She made me feel like I was a part of her family. With the way his family embraced me and seemed to adore me, I actually could see myself being part of this family, too. I was so surprised that I was even feeling like this. It seemed to come out of nowhere. I realized I was actually, and quite unexpectedly, falling in love again.

In the privacy of his room, Corey sat me down and said, "The moment I met you, I knew you were the one. Finding you was hard, but hopefully keeping you will be easy." Then he knelt on one knee, opened a small, black box, looked at me and said, "Will you marry me?"

My soul instantly filled with joy, and tears filled my eyes. I looked at him with the biggest smile and said, "Yes, I will marry you!. He jumped up and gave me the biggest hug and warmest kiss. I was so happy.

On May twenty-fourth the following year, we had a big church wedding with seven bride's maids, seven groomsmen, one maid of honor, one matron of honor, two best men, two flower girls, ring bearer, and a bible bearer. It was the happiest day of my life. My dress was inspired by Cinderella. It was white, wide, with a long train in the back.

Once we were married, I knew the rest of my life was going to be great. I went to work every day but couldn't wait to get home and back in his arms. We were happy like two high school kids in love. Things were good between us. I finally began to exhale and was comfortable with our relationship. I got another position on my job making more money in the banking industry. He was promoted as well as a supervisor over productions, we were living a great life.

Later in our marriage, there were days when Corey would come home stressed out, because of the long nights he had to work, and because of the people he had to deal with. When he was stressed, I always tried to make him feel like a king in his home. When he was settled in his comfortable chair, I took his food to him while he watched television. When we went to bed, I'd make passionate love to him to ease his stress. He talked about having children and I was ready to give him a child.

One morning while getting prepared for work, I was feeling really sick. Suddenly, I had to run to the bathroom to throw up. Corey had already left for work, so I didn't bother to call him. I left the house and went to the local drug store to get a pregnancy test, because my monthly was late. My test came back positive. I was excited, so I called Corey to let him know the news. Corey was excited, too. I couldn't get a doctor's appointment until next week to confirm the pregnancy. That seemed like such a long time to wait, but during those six days Corey treated me like a queen. I didn't have to cook or clean. When I got home from work, he would make sure my bath water was running. It was such an amazing feeling.

Monday came, and it was time to go to the doctor to get tested. I waited in anticipation for the results of my test. The room was cold and getting smaller by the minute, only to find out the test was negative. When I got home to tell Corey the news, I thought he was going to be compassionate, hold me in his arms, and say, *"Baby, it's okay. We will try again."* But he looked at me with such disappointment in his eyes and said, "Can you even get pregnant?" I didn't know what to say or do. I just stared at him and cried.

A week went by, and he barely spoke to me, or touched me. It felt like he was angry with me. So, I politely asked him, "Is everything ok?"

"Yes, I'm fine," he answered. One night, I fixed his food, and brought it to him. He said, "I don't want that." Well, that made me angry, because I had spent my time cooking this meal for him, and for him to say he didn't want it wasn't acceptable. We began to argue. All of a sudden, he pushed me to the floor, and walked away. I was so shocked that I could not move. I couldn't believe he was treating me this way! Did he change towards me because I wasn't pregnant or was he stressing out because of his job? Either way, there was no excuse for being abusive.

We had gotten to the point where I could not say anything to Corey, or he would flip out. If I said, *"Good morning,"* he would glare at me with eyes that seemed to pierce my soul, with an evilness that made a chill run through my body. He was walking around like a ticking time bomb. Corey started shoving me, because I did not allow other girls who he said were his *friends*, to come to my house. The abuse escalated. He started throwing things at me, verbally abusing me, calling me names, such as bitch, and saying you are not a real woman because you cannot give me a baby. I was not sure what was going on. How could someone so sweet turn out to be someone so sour? I began to wonder if I had a sign on my head that said, "ABUSE HER! ABUSE HER!"

I finally decided to talk to his mom about what Corey was doing. She said that he had a temper, but she thought he had outgrown it. She encouraged me to hang in there and said it will get better. I didn't know what to do. I didn't know if I should leave or stay. I thought I was healed from those negative feelings of rejection, being unloved, unwanted, and physically abused, but those feeling came back along with more emotions, including embarrassment, low self-esteem, and emotional abuse.

After one altercation, Corey went to his truck to get his gun, because I had called my uncle to come get me. I had had enough of his abusive mouth and was tired of him throwing me around in our home. But I quickly changed my mind and called my uncle back and told him not to come. I did not want to get him killed. I waited until Corey went to sleep and quietly slipped out the house with just the clothes on my back. I went to my aunt's house and vowed to never go back. I was not going to live like that. He called me the next day and apologized for his behavior. He told me how much he loved me and needed me. He could be so charming, and since he was really sorry for what he did, I went back, because I wanted my marriage to work.

# TRYING TO ESCAPE

We were parked in front of my house and I grabbed all the bags from our shopping trip. Before we got to the door, Santos said, "Madelene you went through a lot of the same things I did, but you don't look like what you have been through."

I smiled and nodded in agreement. "Let's go in. It's been a long day. I walked in the house and kissed my husband and kids.

I walked Santos to the guest house to help her get settled. She took her clothes out of the bags and hung them in the closet. Santos said, "Thanks again for helping me, Madelene. But you never told me how you escaped that situation and how you got here to this happy place."

"Santos, it was still an ongoing abusive relationship. Corey continued to slap me and stomp on me for no reason at all. I was beginning to think that my life was supposed to be a life of hurt, pain, and abuse. Each time he abused me, I would run to a hotel instead of to my family or a friend's, because I didn't want anyone to know what I was going through. I was putting up a front in the presence of my family, because they had told me if he hit me again, they were going to call the cops. So, I didn't tell them. Eventually he apologized and asked me to come back home. He always promised things would be different. We would go to church together and make love as if nothing happened. I forgave him plenty of times."

"Finally, I got pregnant, and that was the happiest day of our lives. He treated me like I was Queen Elizabeth. I didn't have to cook or clean. After work, he told me to just relax until he got home, and he would take care of everything. We went out every weekend spending quality time together. When I started showing, he would talk to my stomach, and tell our son that he could not wait to meet him. It was the most wonderful feeling ever. I loved the way he showed me off to his friends. He was quite funny, because he would say, 'That is my baby y'all.' The day I gave birth to our first child, he ran around the hospital yelling, 'I got a son. I can't believe I have a son.'"

That day the world changed for us. The doctor passed me the baby, but before I could take him, Corey grabbed our son and began to talk to him. It was the most precious moment. When we got home, I did not have anything to worry about. He called my mom, his sisters, and his mom, and gave them daily assignments on how to take care of me and our son. They thought he was overdoing it, but I thought in my mind, maybe this baby will make a difference, maybe we will go back to being happy again. But I was wrong! The abuse didn't stop.

With me being a new mom, I had to learn how to balance my life as a mom and wife. It was difficult trying to remember to take care of everything. For example, once I had forgotten to pay the light bill, and our power was going to be turned off. I called Corey to let him know. When he got home, he was very angry, and yelled, "PUT THE BABY DOWN NOW!"

"No, I'm not going to put the baby down," I said in a timidly. I picked up the phone to call his mom, hoping she could calm him down.

This made him even angrier. He snatched the phone out my hand, looked me in my eyes, and said, "I hate you! I'm going to stay at a friend's house tonight."

That night, I held my baby tight, and whispered in his ear, "I am not going to let nothing or no one hurt you."

You see, Santos, in public he acted like a good husband, and a good father. Neither of us wanted anyone to know the truth. Both of us were leaders in the church, and we valued our reputations, because we were looked upon as role models.

After things calmed down, he came home, and we worked it out again. Love sometimes makes you do stupid things. I decided to go back to work to help him out, because he seemed to be struggling with the bills. Our money was tight, and we could not afford to pay for childcare for our son while I was at work. So, our godmother volunteered to help out with keeping our son. This helped take some pressure off of us while we worked

The following week, we got into another altercation because I came home late from work. I had a job that at times required I had to stay late without notice. I came in the house with the baby in my arms, and he said very angrily to put the baby down. I knew what was going to happen, so I refused to lay the baby down. I clutched the baby tighter to me. When he went in the bedroom, I ran to the car, put the baby in the car, and drove away. He got into his car and chased me up and down the street. I was so afraid, not knowing what to do. I didn't want to call the cops, because I always believed I shouldn't get them involved. So, I drove to a family member's home.

As time went on, Corey, once again, charmed me into coming home. He told me he needed me. Things seemed to be going great after that last incident, so, I had two more babies. We were happy and prospering. We were both in church doing good and getting along really well. By this time, we had five children. But, over time, he began to show signs of cheating. I was not positive, but I had a gut feeling. One day I was coming home from work, I passed the mailbox. Corey always checked the mail. He would get a bad attitude if I checked it. But this particular time as I was driving past the mailbox, a small, still voice told me to check the mail, but I didn't. As I got closer to the house, my stomach started hurting, and that still, small voice told me to go back to the mailbox. So, I went back. My stomach began to feel better. I opened the mailbox, and there were four pieces of mail, all for Corey. When I got in the house, I placed the mail on the table and walked away. That still, small voice said to open the mail, but I was reluctant to do so, because Corey would always fuss at me for opening his mail. I didn't and walked away, but my stomach started hurting again. It was unexplainable. I turned around, walked back to the table, and opened the mail. It was Corey's bank statement. he was the type of husband that believed in separate everything, especially when it came down to our finances. When I opened his bank statement, there were charges from Edible Arrangements, and from a restaurant with an amount indicating that it was for two people. I was in a rage.

A small, still voice prompted me to go to the broken-down car that was in the backyard and search for something, but I didn't know what. While looking around, I found a gift bag with a brand-new outfit, candy, and deodorant. I stormed in the house and got a razor and sliced up the clothes. I smashed the candy and smeared the deodorant all over his new clothes. I was going to make sure he knew that I knew. Nothing was going to stop me from finding out the truth, even though, I already knew.

When Corey got home, I was sitting on the couch waiting like a parent who was waiting for a child who had broken curfew. When the door opened, he didn't have a chance to say hello. I bombarded him with questions, "Corey, who brought you those clothes that are in the broken-down car in the back yard? Who did you buy those edible arrangements for, because I sure didn't get it? And, why does your bank statement show that you paid for dinner for two people?"

"I bought the edible arrangements for my dad to taste before I surprised you with it for Valentine's Day." Of course, I knew he was lying, because it was March.

"I ate alone," he continued to lie.

But I knew better. "What about the clothes in the car?" I asked.

"Oh, I was holding them for a friend."

I said, "Corey, do I look stupid?"

He got angry and yelled, "YOU HEARD WHAT I SAID!"

I walked away to pray to God and asked Him not to let me look like a fool again. I had given Corey chance after chance.

We were not getting along. What made matters worse, was that I was totally dependent on Corey financially. I didn't make much money, even though I had gotten a raise and promotion. The money I made, went to the bills and to our Godmother for daycare fees. He was not the type of person that believed in combining everything together. He would always say, "You got yours, and I got mine." Whenever I asked to borrow money from him, on my next pay day, he demanded me I pay him back. I was so broke, I had to shop for clothes in my aunt's closet, because I didn't have enough money to buy myself anything new. In fact, my family began to talk about me. They said I seemed to have lost my identity since I've been with him. He was very bossy and demanding. Other times, he would give me the silent treatment I walked around like a puppet, not a partner. I was in such a vulnerable position, because I had five children, and I didn't want to disrupt their lives in any way. So, I put that incident of the lying about clothes in the car, edible arrangements, and the dinner under the rug.

The straw that broke the camel's back, was when Corey went on a trip with some people I didn't know. He was gone for three days without very little contact. When he came home, he gave me a list of demands, "Listen, since we only have two weeks of vacation on our jobs, we are going to start vacationing differently. One week, we will vacation with the children, and the other week, we will vacation alone. I'll go my way, and you go your way. Finally, you are going to start paying more bills."

I was in disbelief, because I was already broke. My coworkers were buying me lunch every day; I had no money. I refused and stood my ground, "No, I will not agree to your demands." He started treating me as if I was not good enough for him. One day, I heard him on the phone telling someone that he was just with me because of the kids, but there was no love anymore.

The next week, I asked him if I could borrow some money. As always, he would tell me he wanted his money back. I agreed that I would pay him back by Friday. Well, Friday came, and we were planning to go out of town, but I had to work late. He kept calling my job, but I could not get off early. When I finally got home and pulled in the driveway, he was there waiting on me, with the kids standing next to him. He snatched the car door open, grabbed my phone, threw it down, and broke it. Then, he picked up my pocketbook, and shouted, "Give me my money!"

Our children started screaming and crying, saying, "Mom, just give him the money." With tears in my eyes, I gave him the money and went in the house.

Our five children stayed outside, afraid to come in when they saw him follow me into the house yelling, and spitting in my face, and calling me names. Then, he went to grab a knife. I wasn't sure what he was going to do with the knife. I just stood still with my eyes closed, because my feet would not move. He flipped the couches over in a rage and came toward me with the knife. I was scared! I thought that tonight was going to be the last time I saw my children, and the last time they saw their mommy alive.

Just the week prior, my cousin's husband sliced her neck with a knife, and she was in the hospital fighting for her life. With fear in my eyes, I prayed to God that Corey would put the knife down. He held the knife out towards me as if he was going to stab me. Then, he confused me by placing the knife in my hands, and said, "Stab me! Stab me!" I threw the knife to the floor. I was just perplexed and frightened. When he saw I wasn't going to do it, he turned and walked away. He opened the front door and yelled, "Kids, get in the car." Thankfully, they were still outside and didn't have a clue what was going on in the house. Corey turned and looked at me with hate in his eyes and said, "I am going to divorce you." Then, he walked to the car, got in, and drove off with the children. He took them out of town without me, leaving me lonely, and in pain.

I was trying to figure out what had just transpired. I was in disbelief of how my life was going. The only thing I could do was pray; pray for relief during this storm. I thought to myself that I was not going to let anyone hurt me ever again. Either we were going to get along and be a happy family, or we needed to go our separate ways.

After the weekend was over, Corey brought the kids home, and he left again without telling me where he was going. I noticed that he brought his dirty clothes home and put them in the laundry room. Then, he grabbed some clean clothes to take with him. I was thinking, *"Who is going to clean his dirty clothes?"* That night after talking to my children and putting them in the bed, I threw his clothes away.

After a couple of months had gone by, Corey called and said, "Can I come home? I finally realize that my family means the world to me. I admit I made some bad decisions when I was disrespecting and abusing you over the years."

I thought to myself, *"That whoever you left me for must have found out how many kids you have, and that most of your money was going to us. She probably left him."* So, my stupid self said, "Ok, you can come home." We decided to try again, for the children's sake. This only lasted a year before abuse and cheating started again. I decided to take him to dinner to discuss our marriage. I was trying hard for us to reconcile, but he was not interested or concerned. He sat there on his phone and ignored everything I said to him. He wanted to be free to live his life. Once again, I fell for a fool.

On the way home, I asked him, "Do you want our marriage to work? We have a lot together. We have five precious children who deserve a mother and a father who love each other." We had been married about ten years. Even though I was tired of the abuse I had taken for years, I didn't know how I was going to make it without him. He continued ignoring me, so, I blurted out, "I know you have someone else. Either you are going to leave her or me, because you cannot have us both! Or, I'll leave you!"

Corey looked at me and said, "If you leave me, I will be ok. I don't care about anyone, not even myself." As he drove toward the bridge, he glared at me with rage in his eyes, and the car began to speed up faster.

I looked over at the speedometer. It quickly went from sixty miles per hour to seventy, then eighty miles per hour. My heart began racing! I said, "Corey, slow down! You are going to kill us!"

"I could drive off this bridge, because I don't care about myself or you, anymore." A still, small voice told me to be quiet and you will live. So, I didn't say another word.

Once Corey was calm, he slowed the car down. He said, "I have moved on and I am going to file for divorce."

I was silent for a few minutes, but finally said, "I've had enough this time. You will get your divorce." When we got home, we went to sleep in separate beds. I was laying down with my daughter but was couldn't sleep.

That night was the beginning of a change for me. I vowed that I was not going to be anyone's fool again. I wrote down the names of all the men that had abused me and talked to them as if they were in front of me. I told them that because of them, I was now married to an abuser, but I was not going to take it anymore. I told them that I forgive them, because I had to get strength to live for me and my children. Their spirits will no longer be a part of my life. It will not be dormant, but it will be gone forever. I was tired.

The next morning, I noticed that my husband had already left for work. I packed up the children and moved in with my mother until the divorce was final. I had finally decided that it was time to get some help, because I didn't want to bleed negativity or hurt onto my children. I signed up for psychological counseling at my church. I was blessed to be a part of a church that offered not only spiritual healing, but professional help in all areas of my life. It was time for me to move forward and be restored. It was one thing for me to be hurt and alone, but it was a whole new level since I had children who I loved with all my heart. I didn't want them to experience a defeated life because of my negativity. I wanted them to always speak positive and have a victorious life, if possible.

# SECTION II

# HER

# H E R

# ENOUGH IS ENOUGH, THE MIRROR TOLD THE TRUTH

One day while I was getting ready for work, I looked in the mirror. My inner thoughts said to me, "You are so beautiful." I had enough of thinking the mirror lied. So, I said to myself, *"Yes, I am beautiful. Yes, I am worth something. Yes, I am loved."* I called out from work that day. I sent the children to school, because I felt as if I had to get myself together. I was now divorced, hurt, and damaged. I no longer wanted to go to work or anywhere acting phony, acting whole, acting like superwomen, but on the inside, I was hiding under a cover, because of the abuse and rejection I had gone through. I was so tired of feeling defeated.

I sat down and cried to my Lord and Savior Jesus Christ. I felt like the blind man in the bible who had been deaf and could not talk whom the people brought to Jesus to place his hand on him. Jesus took him aside, away from the crowd, put his finger in the man's ears. Then spit and touched the man's tongue. He looked up to heaven and said Ephphatha, which means "Be Opened" (Mark 7:31-37). With all the negative experiences I went through, each experience caused me to isolate myself from people and suffer in silence. It was weighing me down. Enough of feeling deaf and dumb. I needed an Ephphatha experience. I needed to be opened mentally and physically. Relationships do have their ups and down, but enough of the down spiraling. It was time for me to be opened in order to be completely healed.

It may have looked strange, but I went to the mirror and said, "Ephphatha." I went to my bank and pointed to the ATM machine with my check book in front of it, and said, "Ephphatha, I need God to open every area of my life."

As time passed, I began to feel embarrassment fill my heart, but I refused to feel the shame of letting my ex-husband and other men abuse me the way I allowed them to. I was determined to no longer be a prison of the things that happened to me in the past. I had to learn that my past was a lesson or a testimony not a prison sentence. I felt led to read Romans 8:31-37.

What shall we then say to these things? If God be for us, who can be against us? He that spared not his own, but delivered him up for us all, how shall he not with him also freely give us all things? Who shall lay anything to the charge of god's elect? It is God that justifieth. Who is he that condemneth? It is Christ that died, yea rather, that is risen again, whi is even at the right hand of God, who also maketh intercession for us. Who shall separate us from the love of Christ? Shall tribulation, or distress, or persecution, or famine, or nakedness, or peril, or sword? As it is written, for thy sake we are killed all the day long; we are accounted as sheep for the slaughter, nay, in all these things we are more than conquerors through him that loved us.

After I read that, the spirit jumped up in me with joy. I now had a fight in me that I had never had before, the fight was for my life. I kept telling myself that I am a conqueror, I am more than a conqueror. The past will not steal my future. I will be happy. I will be whole.

As I kept reading different scriptures to encourage myself, I found Psalms 139:14, "I will praise thee: for I am fearfully and wonderfully made: marvelous are thy works; and that my soul knoweth right well." I looked in the mirror again and said, "I am fearfully and wonderfully made, and I am marvelously made. From my hair, hips and fingertips, I was wonderfully made. From my tears to my fears I am wonderfully made, from my abuse to my rejections I am wonderfully made." I was now at the point where I was no longer going to let my past stop me from being all God created me to be. I was determined to do like it says in Philippians 3:13-14, "To forget those things which are behind, and reach for those things which are before me. I'm going to press–toward the mark of the high calling in Jesus Christ."

Since I was the new HER, the HER who loved myself, the HER who protected myself, the HER who is healed and is precious, I decided that I needed a whole make over. I went to the hair salon and got my hair cut and dyed jet black. I went to my favorite store, New York and Company, and bought a couple of new outfits. I went to a spa to get a head-to-toe massage, it felt so good to lay down and receive a deeply relaxing massage. When the massage therapist put the warm blended rich herbal oils on me, I thought I was in heaven. I was tensed up from all that drama with my husband, but in that moment, the tension in my muscles that was caused by emotional and physical stress, was released. I fell asleep when she placed the heated stones on down my back, on my legs, and between my toes. I love a good massage.

I even took myself out to eat and enjoyed reading a book and spending time with myself. I was beginning to feel amazing. Evidently my confidence was showing, because I noticed that I was catching the attention from guys around me, and one even wanted to sit and eat with me, but I turned him down, because I was finally happy trying to find myself. I felt free from my past. I had a glow on my face so bright that even the sun in the sky needed sunglasses.

All of these years I tried to get this feeling, but it took another failed relationship, another love of my life to reject me, and abuse me, that caused me to spiral down into a pit, only to look up and ask God for help. He reached out his hands to pull me out of the pit. Now, I was finally headed to the place of joy, peace, and happiness with my five children. Everything around me seemed new. It was like my eyes were opened for the first time, like in Mark 7:34, "Ephphatha," which means "Be opened" to beautiful things. The grass seemed greener; the sky seemed bluer. The joy I had was overflowing into every area of my life.

I had worked on my current job for so many years, so, after taking some training courses, I applied for another job and got it after the first interview. There is nothing that's going to stop me now. I felt like a qualified woman. Even my children noticed the change in me, that I was glowing. If I was to ever date again, the man in my life would get a whole woman, not a broken-down woman searching for a physical man to rescue and heal me, because that was not his job. That was the job of Jesus Christ.

Santos looked at me and said, "Wow, you don't look like what you've been through."

"I know, because I pursued until I saw HER healed, evolved, restored, delivered, set free, respected, accepted by Jesus, loved, successful, happy, victorious, confident and beautiful," I said.

Because the ME (the person I was), was damaged, imprisoned, bound, abused, rejected, unloved, unsuccessful, sad, defeated, mean, ugly, doubtful, sinful, and in fear. That person was on the verge of suicide and destruction. I told Santos that all it took was for me to see the HER that I wanted to be, because I was fed up with the ME that I was. This may be a little confusing, so let me make a chart so you will fully understand." So, I picked up a tablet and pen, made a chart, and explained what I meant:

| M.E.-This is who I was! | H.E.R.-This is who God created me to be! |
|---|---|
| **M** means I was a **mess** | **H** means **healed** by God |
| **E** means I was **Enclosed** | **E** means **evolved** into the new |
| | **R** means **restored** |
| **Abused** by many | **Complimented** by plenty |
| **Damaged** internally | **Improved** internally |
| **Imprisoned** by attention | **Delivered** from needing attention |
| **Bound** by guilt | **Set free** from shame |
| **Rejected** by people | **Accepted** by God |
| Feeling **Unloved** | Feeling **Loved** |
| **Unsuccessful** | **Successful** |
| **Sad** and **hateful** | **Happy** and **joyful** |
| **Defeated** by trials | Living **Victoriously** |
| **Mean** and **evil** | **Nice** and **forgiving** |
| **Ugly** on the inside | **Beautiful** on the inside and outside |
| **Doubtful** about my future | **Confident** my future will be bright |
| **Fear** of men | **Trust** in God |
| **Sin is** binding | **Jesus** releases |

"The past had stolen so much from me, and I was no longer going to let it stop me from the blessings God had in store for me," I said. "I am not going to stop pursuing ME until I see HER. John 10:10 reads, 'The devil came not, but for to steal, and to kill, and to destroy; I am come that they might have life, and that they might have it more abundantly.' I wanted that abundant life the bible talks about, that abundant life that other people seemed to have, that joy and peace that I witnessed only when I was with my family. Now, I am finally living in it. Once you have had enough of being defeated, enough of walking around unhappy, enough of taking your anger out on your family, enough of being alone, enough of being bitter, you have to make that tough decision. I wanted to live victoriously, wanted love in my life, wanted to be free of being ME, and wanted to be HER, but she seemed so hard to get to. I cried so often, because I could see HER, taste HER, dream about HER, but I didn't know how to get to HER. Like me, you will eventually come to the realization that the only person that can stop you from being blessed is you."

Santos lifted up her hands in a surrender position and declared loudly, "I WANT TO KNOW WHAT IT FEELS LIKE TO BE FREE OF DRAMA. I WANT TO BE HAPPY. I WANT TO BE MADE WHOLE."

I smiled and said, "Santos, it takes time and determination, but you can be made whole. You know, I thank God for what I've gone through. If I hadn't been raped, abused, rejected, neglected, hurt, and divorced, then I would not have had the strength to fight for my life, and live for my children, myself, my new husband, but most of all, for Jesus Christ. I didn't think I would see this day of redemption in Jesus Christ for myself, but now I can witness to what the bible says in Ephesians 3:20, 'God is able to do exceedingly abundantly above all that we can ask or think, according to the power that worketh in us.' The trials and tribulation that I endured, pushed me to pursue greatness for my life, pushed me to want a change, pushed me to want to live, pushed me to want to love myself, and pushed me to pursue ME until I saw HER."

Shirlene said, "Madelene, I am so glad you found yourself. I would have never thought you were an abuse victim because of your strength today."

"You put yourself together nicely," Santos said. "I am going to get there one day."

I said, "Everyone has a story to tell. Some great, some small, but there is a story. And because of my story, I created this motto: Don't judge me because of my past or present, because you don't know my future."

Both girls said "Wow! That's powerful."

Since it was getting late and we were preparing to go to church, I asked Santos if I could pray with her, and she agreed.

"Father God, in the name of Jesus, it is at your name that every knee will bow, and every tongue will confess that you are God. It is at your name the demons begin to tremble and flee. Father, it is at your name that we are set free and are healed! Father, I thank you for your grace and mercy. I thank you for carrying us through. Lord, I thank you for restoring us. God, I thank you for covering us on our life's journey and the road to deliverance. Jesus, we surrender to your will for our lives and release this hurt to you. You said in your word that if we cast our cares upon you, Jesus, you will care for us. You said, take my yoke upon you and learn from me, for I am gentle and humble in heart, and you will find rest for soul. Lord, fill us with your Holy Spirit. Lord, I praise your name because your name is worthy to be praised. Now, Lord I ask that you protect my new friend, Santos, and give her guidance to what lies ahead of her. Give her the comfort she needs to know that you are in control and that you will be with her everywhere she goes. Bless her, but please don't forget about your servant. In Jesus name, Amen."

"Goodnight, Santos.

Santos said, "Goodnight, Madelene."

I walked Shirlene to her car. She hugged me and said, "You are an amazing woman, and I pray that God grant you all the desires of your heart."

"Thanks, girl! Drive safely! See you later," I replied as she got in the car and drove away.

Sunday morning, we went to church. The pastor preached on the topic, "God Will Restore, from Joel 2:25-32, New King James Version, which says, "So, I will restore to you the years that the swarming locust has eaten, the crawling locust, the consuming locust, and the chewing locust, my great army which I sent among you. You shall eat in plenty and be satisfied, and praise the name of the lord your God, who has dealt wondrously with you; and my people shall never be put to shame." It was a great and an on-time message for what Santos was going through. Santos and I went up for alter call, after the sermon. I was praying that God would work a miracle for her and give her peace of mind.

After church, we went back to my home and ate Sunday dinner. Later, I checked my phone messages and found that Dr. Brown had left me a voice message stating she had to kick one of the ladies out of the program, because she had broken the rules for the third time. Now, she had space for Santos. We were so excited for her next journey. We rose up early the next morning to make the long drive to the shelter which was two hours away. During the drive, Santos kept thanking me for coming into her life, and helping her in pursuing ME until she saw herself. Santos said, "I see how happy and at peace you are, so I know that it's possible for me to be happy. It seems as if I've been in prison after being beaten by my husband for years," she said, "But, the next time he hears from me, it will be in court."

I said, "Good for you, because God believes in restoration!"

It was bittersweet to see Santos go, because we had become friends in such a short period of time, but I had done all I could for her. She needs to deal with some internal things that I could not offer help with. Sometimes people try to self-heal like I did, but that only brings more misery. Some people go to church and praise their way through situations, which is the right way. However, there is nothing wrong with seeking professional help for some emotional things.

I smiled and said, "Goodbye, Santos."

As she walked toward the gate, she said, "No, ma'am! Until we see each other again."

"We will always be friends," I reassured her. I watched Santos as she opened the door to the shelter. She turned around one last time and waved at me with a big smile on her face. I know that once she leaves here, she will never be the same again. She will be the new H.E.R.

**The End**

# RESOURCES

If you are in an abusive relationship, please call someone for help. There is no need to suffer in silence.

National Domestic Violence Hotline 1-800-799-7233

Local Police Department

Rape, Abuse, and Incest National Network (RAINN) 800-656-HOPE

# ABOUT THE AUTHOR

Elder Stacci Scott McElveen was born in Brooklyn, New York, to the late Deacon Gary Brown and Evangelist Brown. She is happily married to Leroy McElveen Jr. They have a blended family of three wonderful men, Master Leroy (Nyqwesha) McElveen, Master Victor Scott Jr, and Master Joshua Scott, and a grandson, Jayce McElveen, along with one special god-son, Cinique Johnson, and two special god-daughters, Yatta Gayflor and Naomi Swinton.

Elder McElveen graduated with a Bachelor Degree in Business Science at Limestone College and an Associate Degree in Liberal Arts at Kingsborough Community College.

Elder McElveen is an author and founder of a nonprofit organization called Pursue Me Until You See Her.

She is a people-oriented servant leader who facilitates workshops and retreats for women who have experienced adversity and affliction, by providing a safe platform for them to pursue Recovery, Reset, and Restore.

Stacci's motto is, "Don't judge me from my past or present, because you don't know my future."

www.ingramcontent.com/pod-product-compliance
Lightning Source LLC
LaVergne TN
LVHW051246080426
835513LV00016B/1760